A GUIDE TO THE
FIVE-FOLD
MINISTRY

LUC NIEBERGALL

Printed in the United States of America

First Edition, 2019

ISBN - 9781072072959

Royal Identity Ministries

TABLE OF CONTENTS

A New Stream

We are living in a remarkable time. All across the world, lives are being transformed by the power and love of God. Bodies are being healed; the tormented are freed. The dead are raised and those once held in bondage are liberated. All of this is a part of God's plan to see that people throughout the earth are impacted by His boundless love. It is a divine plan woven by His very will. A plan in which every one of us plays a significant part.

I am someone who firmly believes in God's ability to speak. That being said, the Lord often speaks to me through a variety of different avenues, one of them being visions. Several years ago, I had a vision that I believe speaks to what the Lord is doing throughout the earth:

In this vision, I was watching many ancient streams as they flowed throughout a grassy landscape. Some streams moved at a quick pace, while others moved slower. There were some streams that were steady, and others that shifted from side to side. I knew in my spirit that these streams symbolized past movements that the Lord had released upon the earth throughout history.

Amongst the mesmerizing streams, I looked down anticipating seeing myself standing in water. Instead, I was surprised to see that I wasn't standing in a stream at all. I was standing upon a dirt floor. Perplexed, I asked Holy Spirit why I wasn't in a stream.

In immediate response, He said, "You are not in a particular stream because I'm calling the church to dig a new trench for a new stream that I am releasing upon the earth."

Right now in the church, there is tremendous anticipation brewing for what the Lord is about to do. Many leaders who I chat with throughout the nations feel as though they are sitting on the edge of their seats, waiting for an extravagant birthing that is about to take place. This birthing has everything to do with the newness of what God is about to release throughout the nations.

To position us for the newness of what God wants to do throughout the earth, I believe He is shifting and aligning us. He's adjusting our perspective. He is releasing revelation that is pivotal for us understand in order to steward what He wants to do. I believe an important change He is bringing to our mindsets has to do with our perspective of conventional ministry. We've often perceived those who stand upon church stages as though they are the ones who are more called than others. Sadly, we have believed that the calling of a pastor, or even a church elder, are more spiritually significant compared to, for example, someone who is called to run a small business.

I've personally had the privilege of travelling the world, training and equipping the church for over a decade. While I consider this a tremendous honour to do so, I understand that what I do isn't necessarily more spiritual or important than someone who is called to work in media, or someone who is called to be a stay at home parent. What I do isn't "better"; it's simply different. Each of us carry the responsibility of stewarding our platform God has given us with humility, excellence, and uprightness of heart.

With all my heart, I believe we are living in a time where the pulpit and pew separation in the church is coming to a distinct close. Believing that it is more radical or spiritual to lead from behind a pulpit, compared to leading in business, government, the arts, etc, is a flawed mentality. Many of my friends who greatly challenge me with their radical passion for God's kingdom are not in conventional ministry. They stand as beacons of light in business, government, the education system, church, family, arts/entertainment, and media. God is raising up a kingdom army that demonstrates His love in every vein of society.

Every one of us is called to do remarkable things for God's kingdom. Many of you who are reading this book may not be called to conventional ministry to have influence with the church. Maybe you're called to teach high school students. Maybe you're called to write songs that inspire hope. No matter what you are called to, God has a plan to impact lives through you in your sphere of influence. In order for this to happen, we need to allow the Lord to train and equip us appropriately.

Take a look at this scripture with me:

Ephesians 4:11-12: "And He Himself gave some to be apostles, some prophets, some evangelists, and some pastors and teachers, for the equipping of the saints for the work of ministry, for the edifying of the body of Christ."

In many church circles apostles, prophets, evangelists, pastors, and teachers are referred to as the five-fold ministry. Biblically, they are an expression of God's leadership. When Jesus walked the earth He was the full embodiment of the five-fold ministry. Jesus is our great Apostle, Prophet, Evangelist, Pastor, and Teacher. When He died, rose again and ascended into heaven, in His wisdom He scattered these five callings into different individuals. I believe His will was that they would function together in one body again; which is the body of Christ.

Not everyone is called to carry one of these five callings. In fact, I would propose there may even be far fewer than we would assume. As stated in this verse, the five-fold ministry is to "equip the saints for the work of ministry." Not all of us carry influence to train and equip the church. Most of us are called to different spheres of influence entirely. However, what we do see here is that the five-fold ministry is called to train the church so that everyone is equipped.

For the sake of practicality, I will give you a quick overview of each office-calling to give you a base knowledge before you go on reading:

Apostle - Apostles are visionaries who receive strategy of what it would look like for heaven to invade earth in a sustained move of God. They function as catalysts and builders to bridge their God-given vision into reality. Their job in the body of Christ is also to train the rest of the church to be apostolic minded. They are to train the church to receive heaven's heart and vision for each individual's entrusted sphere of influence.

Prophet - Prophets have a supernatural grace over their lives to hear and speak the word of God. They will more than likely have the ears of very influential people to speak into, bringing prophetic direction and guidance. A prophet's job within the church is also to train and equip the rest of the church in how to hear and speak the word of the Lord. When this is achieved, every individual in the church becomes a vessel for God's word to be spoken through.

Evangelist - Evangelists have a deep love for those who do not yet know Jesus. They are passion and compassion driven to see the gospel impacting beyond the four walls of the church. One of the primary functions of an evangelist is to train and equip the rest of the church in how to become evangelistic.

Pastor - Pastors have a passion to bring healing to the brokenhearted, so therefore carry a strong anointing to bring restoration to the wounded soul. Pastors also carry a strong revelation of how to live out kingdom relationships. Pastors are gatherers, and lead by doing life with people. A pastor's job within the church is to train and equip the rest of the church in how to become pastoral.

Teacher - Teachers have a grace over their lives to tap into revelatory truths from the written word of God. Since this is the case, teachers have a great focus on teaching and studying so they can train the church to tap into deep truths within scripture. Teachers function by guiding the church in how to live a Christ-like life through biblical teachings. Many teachers also train and equip the church in how to receive revelation from the Bible, as they themselves do.

Each five-fold minister, whether they are an apostle, prophet, evangelist, pastor, or teacher is a gift to the Bride of Christ (the church), commissioned to help beautify her to be pure and spotless before the nations. They accomplish this by equipping the church through their own ministerial expression. Once these different facets of leadership are both restored and received by the church, we will have a well-rounded group of people who can represent Jesus the Apostle, Prophet, Evangelist, Pastor, and Teacher in their appointed spheres of influence.

Choosing to be Well-Rounded

Even though we may not be called to walk in a five-fold office, our giftsets will naturally have a tendency to lean towards one or two of them. You may have observed this with yourself. Maybe you find your friends often coming to you for advice in relationships, since you have such a pastoral heart. Perhaps you are tremendously passionate about diving into the Bible, as a teacher would. Even though we have a tendency to gravitate to certain giftsets, we need to remember to allow ourselves to be trained by every facet of Jesus' leadership.

I remember a few years ago, my wife and I were putting on a school on hearing the voice of God. For several weeks we had about sixty students who were being trained in the prophetic ministry. Leading up to the final week of the school, I announced to the students that for the last night we were going to actually be going out to a nearby train station to practice everything we learned in class. We were going to give prophetic words to those who didn't yet know Jesus.

Being optimistic, I thought everyone would be thrilled! However, on the final night of our school I was blown away as I watched our numbers dwindle from sixty people to six!

Looking back at this moment, I find it quite comical. However, there is a truth we can see in this story. Many people from this group were very comfortable with receiving from Jesus the Prophet. They were comfortable with learning how God speaks. Yet, they felt greatly uncomfortable with Jesus the Evangelist.

As people, we often have a tendency of finding comfort in the familiar. That being said, without even realizing it we will often position ourselves to receive from leaders who have similar giftsets as us. Therefore, we have prophetic people only receiving from prophets; pastoral people who only receiving from pastors, etc. When we compartmentalize how we are receiving from Jesus, we are making the decision to become unbalanced. We may learn to hear God's voice from being around prophets, but we also need to be around pastors to learn about relationships and how to be healthy in our soul. We need to receive from apostles to know how we fit in the grand scheme of God's plan, as well as know how to receive from evangelists to know how to reach those who don't yet know Jesus. Jesus is our great Apostle, Prophet, Evangelist, Pastor, and Teacher even if certain aspects of Him seem foreign to us, or may even make us uncomfortable.

For years in the church we have in many ways gathered around one or two types of leaders; however, when we have done this we have been giving Jesus permission to only minister and build in one or two areas of our lives. We need to be a people who are so hungry to know Him that we will not compartmentalize how we receive Him.

Genesis 1:26: "Then God said, 'Let Us make man in Our image, according to Our likeness.'"

God is a triune being; a Trinity. He is the Father, the Son, and Holy Spirit. Since we are created in the image of God, in the very fabric of who we are, we are also a trinity. We are a three-fold-being made of spirit, soul, and body. I find it interesting how God has gifted the different five-fold offices to minister to different parts of our three-fold being.

In many ways, apostles and prophets function by ministering to the spirit of an individual. These two specific offices bring kingdom vision and activate many of the gifts of the Spirit within the church. They help us to function healthily in our spirit. Pastors and teachers minister to the soul of those in the church. Our soul is our mind, will, and emotions. Pastors have a grace to minister to the heart and emotions of the church, and teachers have a mandate to minister to the mind by training us to renew the way we think. Evangelists minister to the body of those in the church by activating the word of God within us, helping make us mobile.

When we receive training from the five-fold ministry, we are partnering with the Lord to be mature in the fullness of our three-fold being. Not one part of us gets stuck in infancy or adolescence. We grow up, maturing in totality.

I'm going to end this chapter sharing a Bible story with you:

Acts 1:16-26 tells us an intriguing story after, Judas, one of the disciples took his own life. After this event, the eleven remaining apostles came to the conclusion that someone needed to come alongside them in replacement of Judas. The apostles chose two men who had been with them while Jesus walked the earth who they considered worthy of the call to apostleship. These two men were Barsabas and Matthias. They cast lots to see who would fill the abandoned platform and the lot fell on Matthias. This is when God's church government came to a place of wholeness. A blatant gap was filled.

We see right in the next chapter that a great outpouring of the Spirit takes place throughout the early church. It is important to note that before God showed up in such a way and the kingdom began to take reign in the land, that church government needed to be brought into God's order. Since the five-fold ministry is God's selected governing leadership, it being stationed in its proper position within the body of Christ is pivotal for us to see a genuinely advancing move of God.

When the five-fold ministry takes its place of governance in the church to minister, train, and equip we will have individuals who are highly apostolic who are receiving vision for their work places. We will be bold, knowing how to move heaven by faith to influence those around us who do not know Jesus. We will also have pastoral hearts to tend to people's needs. We will be able to prophetically tap into the Father's heart for those who we interact with. We will be unswayable in knowing our mandate, because we are deeply rooted in the written word of God.

We can clearly see that the restoration of these offices functioning in the church plays a crucial part in the end of the pulpit and pew separation. It will demolish the separation of "superstar ministers" and observers, because everyone will be rising to walk in the fullness of their potential. The movement happening on the earth isn't about a select few. It is all inclusive; every one of us playing an important role.

If you're reading this book, you likely fall into one of two categories. The first category is that you might be wondering if you are called to walk in a specific office, or maybe the Lord has already confirmed that you do. In this case, you may be reading desiring to learn more about your function. The second category is that you don't believe you walk in a five-fold ministry office, yet desire to know how to be trained properly by Jesus' different facets of leadership. Either way, my heart is to help demystify a topic that seems confusing and complex, yet is quite simple.

As I previously mentioned, I've been travelling and equipping the church for over a decade. I've had the great privilege of walking in close relationship with many respected five-fold ministers. I've also been a part of several five-fold ministry teams. My goal is to take both my knowledge and experience concerning these five-fold graces, to show you their value and functions. My desire is that God would expand your understanding, that you would encounter these different expressions from His heart.

Pray this prayer with me:

"Jesus, I repent for any time I may have compartmentalized how I've received you. I receive you as my Apostle, Prophet, Evangelist, Pastor, and Teacher. Train me so I may be appropriately equipped to impact the sphere of influence to which you've called me."

OFFICE OF AN APOSTLE

When we choose to walk in an apostolic mindset, we are inviting God to impregnate our heart and mind with His vision for our surroundings. Not only will we begin seeing lives transformed, but the very culture that enshrouds us will begin to reflect the vision God has birthed in our heart. As the global church, if we choose to view our lives as a mission field to apostolically advance the kingdom of God, the glory of God will undoubtedly penetrate every vein of society.

DEFINING AN APOSTLE

I truly believe we are amidst an apostolic reformation in the church. God is transitioning the church from the corner of the field, to the centre stage of the world. He is training the church to not sit on the sidelines, passively watching the world change around us. He is showing us how to stand victoriously in the nations. He is raising us up to walk out our apostolic mandate, to expand the kingdom of God throughout the earth in every stream of society. I believe apostles play a significant role in this movement.

The office of an apostle is a very important part of God's leadership. Yet, due to not understanding the apostolic function we have in many ways overlooked its necessity. Since we have overlooked its necessity, it is an office that in most circles been completely forgotten. This is why I often refer to the apostolic ministry as the *forgotten office of the five-fold ministry*.

I remember when I first gave my heart to the Lord, I was drawn to studying Paul the apostle's ministry. However, since I had a lack of teaching on church leadership, I was unaware of what an apostle actually was. After church one day, I approached my pastor at the time hoping he would shed some light on my current curiosity. I greeted him with what I thought was simple a question by asking him what an apostle was. After asking my question, my pastor looked over at me blankly and responded by saying, "Luc, I honestly have no clue what an apostle is."

Looking back, I find this a rather amusing story, but it shares an interesting element of truth. It's not only this one pastor who doesn't understand this office; I've met many who aren't aware of its meaning. Unfortunately, the office of an apostle is one that in many ways been completely forgotten. This is why the myth which says apostles were only for the early church has crept into some of our doctrines. When really, if we understood the role of the apostolic ministry we would undeniably understand its importance and would be quick to embrace it.

Much of the church has placed the apostolic on the back-burner in our understanding. I don't believe this was done intentionally, but instead due to a lack of revelation and definition concerning the global church's apostolic call. The definition of what it means to be an apostle is actually quite elementary. The word "apostle" translated from the Greek means "sent one". Apostles in the New Testament knew they were sent ones from heaven to bridge the kingdom of heaven to earth. The apostles would birth movements. They would train and equip the masses to move in the love and power of God. They would govern, steward, and mobilize the church to make as big an impact as they could for the gospel's sake.

We are all called to be apostolic to some degree, since we are all "sent ones." What then is the distinction from someone who is "apostolic" compared to one who walks in the office of an apostle? I know of several men and women who I believe walk in the office of an apostle. Based on my experience with such people and what I can see biblically, I believe there are three characteristics that mark someone who truly walks in the office of an apostle:

Apostles Build

When I've met a true apostle, there is an innate ability to build for the Lord. It doesn't matter if they are in what feels like barren land; someone who is truly an apostle will find a way to establish something for the Lord.

1 Corinthians 3:10: "According to the grace of God which was given to me, as a wise master builder I (Paul the apostle) have laid the foundation, and another builds on it. But let each one take heed how he builds on it."

An apostle has the ability to look into the heart of God, to see the blueprint that the Lord wants to establish on the earth. They will then take that blueprint and begin to build it upon the earth.

Therefore, through building, the heartbeat of heaven is established on the earth. While someone who is highly pastoral, loves the individual and dreams for the individual, so does someone who is apostolic. However, apostles don't only dream for the individual, they dream and burn for the masses.

Moses is one of my favourite examples of what it looks like to walk in an apostolic anointing. The Old Testament refers to Moses as being a prophet, which he was; however, I believe if Moses lived in New Testament times that he would be better recognized as an apostle. I have spent a significant amount of time studying Leviticus, Numbers, and Deuteronomy. I know that many people struggle focusing while reading these particular books considering how intricately detailed they are, but there are profound treasures hidden in each. Something we can see in these books is the tremendous apostolic grace that was over Moses' life. Moses' sphere of influence was with the nation of Israel. As an apostolic person, Moses' responsibility was to receive divine vision from God for this nation. Moses needed to tap into the blueprint that resided in God's heart, and bring that into existence within the people of Israel. This is what much of Leviticus, Numbers, and Deuteronomy is; it is the very culture that was in the heart of God for a nation. Of course, Moses' job wasn't only to receive the vision, but to also apostolically build until that culture was in full fruition throughout Israel. While many modern-day apostles receive and establish vision for a network of churches or an organization, Moses was called by God to receive and establish vision for an entire nation.

I have a friend who is very gifted in apostolic building. He is one who looks into the heart of God, and then builds God's desires on the earth. The man is so apostolic that it seems like all he needs to do is sneeze and somehow a church gets planted. Several years ago, he could feel something burning within his heart; it was a desire to see Jesus exalted throughout the nations in every vein of society. What started as him discerning what was in the heart of God, he then began building what he discerned upon the earth. He has now established several churches throughout the world. These churches are brimmed with those in business, government, the arts and entertainment industry, the educational system, etc. Not only is he seeing people impacted in the churches he's planted, but people are being healed, saved, and delivered through those who he has trained and risen up under his leadership. The stories of lives being impacted through this ministry are mind-blowing. All of this began with one man who was courageous enough to not only see what burned in the heart of God, but to also build what was in the heart of God.

Someone who is mature in the apostolic ministry understands that building something for the Lord is far more than just buying a building and setting in motion some good programs. An apostle's job is to form Christ within the church (the people) so they can stretch beyond adolescence and into maturity. It is far less about building a structure, rather than building powerful people. Paul the apostle wrote this:

Galatians 4:19: "My little children, for whom I labour in birth again until Christ is formed in you."

Apostles raise up and surround themselves with powerful people to help establish the vision that burns within God's heart. An apostle is in many ways like a manager of a store. While some people might be an expert in specific areas of the store, their understanding will not stretch beyond their station. An apostle on the other hand, understands the full functioning of every job that makes the store flow and work. Since this is the case, apostles are usually very universally gifted. They also have a grace to weave in and out of specific giftings and anointings if necessary to complete their mandate. Other than Jesus, Paul was arguably the most anointed apostle who has ever walked the earth. Throughout the book of Acts and the Epistles, we can see very clearly how Paul operated as an apostle.

Paul, although an apostle, would often go to a region first functioning in the role of an evangelist. He would preach the gospel, heal the sick, raise the dead, and cast out demons. When people were birthed into salvation, he would then prophetically pick a few who he saw as potential leaders and began to father them. As an expert builder, Paul would build and form Christ within those he was fathering through his teachings, so he could later appoint them within the church. Here, he would begin to operate in more of the giftings of a teacher, and would also pastor those he discipled. As I have said, apostles will often understand the full functioning of what they are building, and will for a time step into different roles when necessary. After a few leaders were risen up under Paul, he would begin to station them within the church he was birthing.

The story of Noah's ark functions as an interesting parallel to the apostolic ministry. This makes sense considering Noah's ark was the first structure in scripture mandated by God to be built by man. The ark is symbolically an excellent parallel of how an apostle is to utilize the church's diversity. Just as Noah built a boat that had a place for every species of animal and its mate, an apostle is to make space for people where their gifts can be used for the kingdom in a way that will bring multiplication. It didn't matter to Noah how different one animal was from the other; he had a place prepared for each within the boat.

1 Peter 2:5: "You also, like living stones, are being built into a spiritual house to be a holy priesthood, offering spiritual sacrifices acceptable to God through Jesus Christ."

It is interesting to note that we are not called to be "living bricks" to build a spiritual house, but instead are called as living stones. Bricks are easy to place on top of one another because they are in the shape of rectangles, while stones come in all shapes and sizes. It takes an expert to put a variety of awkwardly-shaped stones together with the intent of seeing them work together for a common purpose. An apostle knows that there is a place in the body of Christ for every gift, calling, mantle, anointing, and talent. As people are released by the apostle to minister in whatever area they are called, more ministries and leaders will begin to pop up, expanding the vision. In doing this, the people as a whole become a massive bridge that usher heaven to earth in the realm where they are anointed to function.

Apostles live to see what is happening in heaven established on the earth. An apostle steps into seemingly barren land, and creates a dwelling place for God that is made of living stones from the foundation, right to the top. At first, things look messy and the apostle is running around trying to make everything work, but in the end after everyone is raised up and appointed, they get to step back and see an organic wineskin functioning and operating on its own. Essentially, the apostle works himself or herself out of a job, so they can potentially begin to build elsewhere. When an apostle is present, those who lead under their accountability will begin to flow in an apostolic anointing to manage and steward. This is essential, otherwise all of the ministries that were birthed through the apostle remain co-dependent on him or her, instead of becoming self-sustaining. Although apostles may begin building in another place, they will often take a position of governing and overseeing the move of God that was set in motion through them. We can see how even though Paul planted in many different places, he was constantly writing the churches and playing the role of a father to the churches he had raised up.

Without common-day apostles working within the church, the body of Christ will go without proper governing and order. The presence of an apostle deposits a sense of purpose, since they carry a revelation that everyone has a place in God's kingdom.

Apostles Carry a Realm of the Supernatural

1 Corinthians 12:12: "Truly the signs of an apostle were accomplished among you with all perseverance, in signs and wonders and mighty deeds."

I find this characteristic a very important one for apostles. The reason being, if an apostle were simply one who is a builder, then every business leader would be referred to as an apostle. Remember, an apostle isn't only a builder; they are a "sent one". Where are they sent from? They are sent from heaven to earth, to establish the culture of heaven on earth through building. That being said, while apostles can have a tendency of being business-minded, scripture tells us that supernatural fruit is also one of the marks of an apostle. When an apostle builds something from the heart of heaven, heaven's culture will be present.

I often add a specific excerpt from the first book I ever wrote called, "Reigning as Royalty," to my writings because I believe it's a good description of the kingdom of heaven. I decided to add it here because I believe it articulates what an apostle establishes through building. If you have read through this excerpt before in previous books, I would encourage you to read over it again. Something powerful happens when we choose to renew our mind in truth. Sometimes this takes repetition.

"We will start off in Luke 11:2-4. Tradition tells us that this is the Lord's prayer, however it is important to note that Jesus wasn't even praying; He was instead teaching His disciples how they ought to pray. When Jesus' disciples came

to ask Him how they should talk to the Father He spoke and said, 'When you pray, say: Our Father in heaven, Hallowed be thy name. Your kingdom come. Your will be done on earth as it is in heaven.' The word 'kingdom' that Jesus referred to here literally means 'kings domain'. If the kingdom is God's domain, then we know that wherever the kingdom of heaven is, that's where God is - it is His dwelling place. The culture of a household is always a reflection of the culture or personality of the One who has headship over it. Since God is heaven's creator, He is the head and authority of heaven which is His house. God in His very being is goodness and love. If heaven was God's expression in creation, we can be sure that its culture is a direct reflection of who God is.

"Look back at what Jesus says in verse 2, 'On earth as it is in heaven.' Jesus was literally telling His disciples to pray that whatever was going on in heaven would be made manifest on earth. Jesus came to release a revelation that it was God's heart desire for the perfection of the culture of heaven to co-exist with creation on earth. Many of us have gotten off track in Jesus' true Kingdom message. A lot of us are living to see and experience heaven one day when we die, when it was Jesus' desire for us to experience the blessings of heaven now while we are still on earth. Ephesians 1:3 says, 'Blessed be the God and Father of our Lord Jesus Christ, who has blessed us with every spiritual blessing in the heavenly places in Christ.' This doesn't say that He will 'eventually' bless us with every spiritual blessing in heaven, it says He already has. He said, 'repent for the kingdom of heaven is at hand' (Matthew 4:17) saying that it is an

attainable and tangible kingdom in hand's grasp. Heaven is in hand's grasp! This is good news! Jesus came to establish on earth a heavenly kingdom which functions out of heavenly principals here and now in our lives.

"What are some principles of heaven? We know that the Bible says that in heaven there is no sickness, no disease, no depression, addictions, or poverty. There is only perfect love, perfect health, peace, joy, and abundant blessing. The kingdom of heaven is a place where God's will has complete rule and reign. When we receive Jesus as King we come under the rule and principals of His kingdom. We actually become citizens of heaven (Philippians 3:20). Sickness and addictions have no authority over us because they don't even exist in the kingdom that we are from. The Bible talks about two kingdoms; the kingdom of heaven (which is the kingdom of God) and the kingdom of darkness. When two kingdoms collide the greater kingdom will always prevail. A good example would be, say, if the kingdom of darkness had rule in an area of someone's life where they struggled with something like depression. When they receive Jesus as King in this area of their heart, His kingdom comes which is filled with perfect joy. Since God's kingdom is greater than the kingdom of darkness, His kingdom casts away depression, and joy becomes established in the individual's life."

- Reigning as Royalty

What an apostle builds won't only have the mark of excellence. It will have the very mark of heaven. An apostle building, bridges heaven to earth so that the principles of the kingdom of God are established among us. When I look at any seasoned apostle, their ministry is saturated with the supernatural love of God. The sick are healed. Those in bondage are set free. Addictions are loosed. Those who don't know Jesus come to know Him. People are supernaturally equipped to live out their destinies.

Apostles Equip and Release

I personally believe true apostles are quite rare. In fact, with all the travelling and ministering I've done, I believe I've met very few who I could confidently say carry such a calling. What we need to understand is that while few of us are called to walk in the office of an apostle, every single one of us is called to be apostolic in our spheres of influence. This doesn't necessarily make us apostles; it makes us apostolic. It doesn't matter who we are in the body of Christ, we are called to be apostolically minded for the kingdom of God.

Ephesians 4:11-12: "And He Himself gave some to be apostles, some prophets, some evangelists, and some pastors and teachers, for the equipping of the saints for the work of ministry, for the edifying of the body of Christ."

Apostles function to train and equip us to be apostolically minded. A seasoned apostle understands that those around them aren't called to only serve their vision. A true apostle recognizes that those around them all have spheres of influence that God's heart burns to impact.

One of my good friends who I believe carries the calling of an apostle, doesn't only build, but spends much time teaching others to build. He spends time investing into significant business leaders, celebrities, those in government, and other apostolic leaders. Through mentorship, he doesn't only guide them as a prophet would, he trains them to build the heart of heaven in their arenas of influence. He is an apostle who is training others to build the way an apostle would. He is training them by shaping within them an apostolic mindset.

Many people believe the first apostolic commissioning happened when Jesus sent out the seventy in Luke 10. However, I believe it happened long before that. I believe it was given when God said to Adam and Eve in Genesis 1:28, "Be fruitful and multiply; fill the earth and subdue it; have dominion over the fish of the sea, over the birds of the air, and over every living thing that moves on the earth."

When Adam and Eve were within the garden of Eden, they were experiencing heaven on earth. They were in a continuous state of revival culture. The garden of Eden was a place where heaven and earth overlapped one another. The garden was literally a habitation place for the kingdom of heaven. Heaven did not just manifest in the garden on special occasions; the garden was heaven's dwelling place to rest. God's kingdom had full reign. *Eden* in the Hebrew tongue is translated, "place of pleasure". When He created Adam and Eve to live in the garden they both lived in perfect love, perfect health, peace, joy, and abundant blessing. They suffered from no ailments because sickness did not exist in this garden. Adam and Eve were flawless. Heaven's principles were all in fruition and a culture of perfection was in effect.

What we need to understand is this: God did not intend for Adam and Eve to only kick back on a spread of grass to soak in this culture for the rest of eternity. There was definitely an aspect where they were called to soak and receive, but there was also a mandate that was given. The mandate was, "Be fruitful and multiply; fill the earth and subdue it; have dominion over the fish of the sea, over the birds of the air, and over every living thing that moves on the earth." Adam and Eve's job was to take this heaven on earth experience which existed within the garden, to expand it to the ends of the earth. This way there wouldn't only be one single garden that was the dwelling place of heaven, but the entire earth would be partnered with the culture of the kingdom of heaven.

Even though Adam and Eve didn't carry the titles, I think it's fair to say that Adam and Eve were in fact the first apostles to walk the earth. They were called to be *sent ones* with a specific vision and mandate from God into the world.

The mandate over every individual's life in the church is much the same as the mandate that was upon Adam and Eve, even though each will have a unique expression catered to their calling. Our job is to take revival that has occurred in our hearts, and to expand the culture of the kingdom of heaven outwards to invade our places of influence wherever we are called.

Some of you who are reading this may be stationed in business or in government. Others of you may be called to the education system, the church, arts, media, the entertainment industry, or family. Just as Adam and Eve were commissioned to multiply the atmosphere of the kingdom of heaven throughout the world, God has called you as a sent one to establish His kingdom wherever you are called. You are called as an apostolic warrior who carries a mission to bring change and freedom to a broken world. Apostles play a key part in preparing us to receive God's blueprint for our spheres of influence so we can build God's kingdom in our places of mandate.

COMMON PITFALLS OF THE APOSTOLIC

The apostolic ministry is an irreplaceable part of God's kingdom. However, if we are going to see it utilized to its full expression, we need to be aware of its potential pitfalls. Just like every ministry, it is beneficial when it is healthy, however it can also cause hurt and pain if it's not wielded with love and integrity. Over the years, I've had friends who are apostles, and those who are highly apostolic. They've helped shed light for me to understand what pitfalls can follow the apostolic ministry. Some of these pitfalls are struggles they've observed with others, as well as some they've personally learned to overcome.

Here are some pitfalls that can be experienced by apostles and those who are highly apostolic:

Building Independently

Apostolic vision is not likely the vision of a minimalist. Apostolic people have a tendency to dream on a grand scale. That being said, in order to see grand vision come to pass, it takes many people to do so. While not all apostolic leaders struggle in this area, some feel as though they need to take on the full burden of seeing their vision come to pass.

Apostles and apostolic people can slip into a mentality of wanting to build on their own for several different reasons. There may be times when an apostolic person needs to plow ahead to build when no one believes in what they are building. This is sometimes the cost of being a forerunner. However, if we are building on our own as a lifestyle, then we need to begin to question why. Here are a few different reasons why apostolic people could slip into independent building:

1. An apostolic person may try to build independently from others because there is a belief that no one else believes in their vision, so therefore feel as though they need to do it alone. As I said, there may be times to diligently build, even when others are not catching the vision. However, sometimes we can slip into building alone simply out of insecurity. Sometimes we will have a vision from the heart of God, yet due to a lack of confidence we will try to establish a vision on our own instead of asking for help. Embracing this type of mindset can easily lead apostolic people into walking in a lone-ranger mentality. Submitting to this level of insecurity will minimize an apostolic person's vision, and will greatly limit their ability to build for God's kingdom. Apostolic people need teams around them if they want to build with excellence.

2. An apostolic person may try to build independently from others due to a mentality of elitism. A mentality of elitism is when someone feels the need to have their hands in every realm of what is being built. This may be possible with a vision that is on a smaller scale; however, as the vision grows this will likely lead to burnout. A posture of elitism is often rooted in pride, believing that the only way something will be built efficiently is if we do it ourselves. This results in others who are participating to feel undermined and devalued. Elitism will often leave an apostolic leader spreading themselves too thin due to not knowing how to delegate. This is the result of fearing giving away authority to others.

3. An apostolic person may try to build independently because of a mentality of perfectionism. While elitism is rooted in pride, perfectionism is often the by-product of anxiety. Often apostolic people who struggle with high levels of perfectionism will feel as though what they are building needs to be perfect, otherwise it reflects poorly on who they are. This often takes place when a leader directly links their worth and value to what they are building. They actually find their identity in what they build, rather than who they are as a son or daughter of God. This results in taking on much more than what is reasonable.

We need to always remember that God has called us to build with one another. When we look at the five-fold ministry, we see how different callings, gift-sets, and personalities were created for the purpose of working together, rather than independently.

Worshipping Vision

We know vision is something that is an important component for the apostolic ministry. Yet, we should never begin to see vision as something bigger than it is. Vision is important; however, it is not something that should be worshipped or idolized. A key sign for knowing if we are stepping into a mentality of worshipping vision would be if we have a greater love for our vision than we do for individuals. If our drive to see our vision established is not moved from a place of loving God and people, then our ambition is likely rooted out of insecurity. This is where we can begin to step into the camp of building for our own kingdom instead of God's.

Vision should never trump people. In fact, if we are believing for a move of God and we prioritize vision before people, then we have already missed the mark. We will have missed the mark because God's vision for revival *is* people. People are not pawns. People are people. This means that just because we have a strategy doesn't give us the right to use others in order to see our plans established. People should always be valued above vision. Period. Every individual deserves to be valued, honoured, and treated as though they are significant, because they are.

A while back, I stumbled upon a very interesting revelation concerning this. Back in the Old Testament kings were born into their kingship through their lineage. All throughout scripture this is true, other than for three kings that I can think of. One of those kings was the people's king, which was Saul. However, the other two were God's hand-chosen kings. These two men were king David, and even though this second man didn't carry the title of a king, he functioned as one. This man was Moses.

Before their kingship, David and Moses actually shared professions. It's interesting to me that God trained both of His handpicked kings as shepherds. This is profound because God trained these two men to learn how to pastor the few, before they could pastor a nation. God wanted to shape within them a pastoral heart. He distilled within them the heart to lay down their lives for the individual before they could have nationwide influence. God taught them to love the individual more than the vision.

I believe God longs for leaders who have their priorities straight. While vision is important, it is never meant to be worshipped. It is never meant to be valued more than people.

Burnout

This pitfall often ties into the last two. Burnout is often followed by building independently and worshipping vision. Often when we slip into a mentality of worshipping vision, we will not be able to separate our vision from ourselves as individuals. This results in us placing our worth and value in what we build, thus allowing it to become all-consuming. This can create a vicious cycle of working excessively to find purpose and value.

This level of burnout is very damaging because it doesn't only effect the one overexerting themselves; it hurts those who they are in relationship with. I have seen many families who have been greatly neglected because a minister finds their identity in what they do, so therefore chooses ministry over family. It's true that there is a great cost for us to walk out our calling; however, that cost should never be connection with our family.

Our priorities in life need to be in the correct biblical order. Our first priority in life needs to be to know the Lord. The most important thing we can do with our lives is to know God as a friend. Our second priority is our family (spouse and children). Thirdly, comes our ministry and career. We cannot reverse God's order of priorities because each priority functions to sow into the following. Our relationships with people cannot be put above our relationship with God because it is our relationship with Him that teaches us to walk in Godly friendships. This means that if there is a flaw in our relationship with the Lord, then there will inevitably be some form of dysfunction in our relationships. It is the same with how our spouse and children are to stand before ministry or career. We will never learn to be a good husband, wife, father, or mother through what we learn in doing ministry. God made family before He made the five-fold ministry. It is being faithful in our relationships with God others that train us to be great leaders in our spheres of influence. We need to take time sowing into them.

Building Prematurely

Apostles and apostolic leaders thrive in building and establishing vision. That being said, if they are in a time of waiting before building, they could wrestle with experiencing restlessness. This could result in trying to run ahead of the Lord to begin building prematurely. This can lead to us self-promoting ourselves out of our seasons of training before God's intended time. It can also result in striving to build in our own strength.

Remember Matthew 17 at the Mount of Transfiguration - Jesus took Peter, James, and John up the mountain where they came into an incredible encounter where heaven overlapped the earth. They could see Elijah and Moses standing there with them as Jesus was transfigured before their eyes into His heavenly form. Peter responds to this encounter in an intriguing way, he says, "Lord, it is good for us to be here; if You wish, let us make here three tabernacles: one for You, one for Moses, and one for Elijah."

The reason why Peter wanted to build tabernacles was because in the Old Testament when the glory of God would come, it would always have to be contained within a tabernacle or tent to be sustained. Being an uprising apostolic leader, Peter instantly went into ministry-mode to try to build, to contain the glory of God so they could try to sustain the kingdom atmosphere they were experiencing. After this, the Father spoke through a bright cloud and said, "This is My beloved Son, in whom I am well pleased. Hear Him!" This reveals that the purpose of Jesus bringing the three onto the mountain was not for them to minister by building tents to contain the glory of God. It was for them to hear from the Father to receive an internal revelation about who Jesus was.

Hiddenness before building is a time of preparation for the builder. God wants to build revelation within the heart of an apostolic person before they build with their hands. When we are building apostolically, what we build with our hands for God's kingdom will always be a reflection of what we have allowed God to build in our heart. If we have a culture of internal health within our soul, there will be health in the soul of what we build. If we have a personal revelation of kingdom relationships, that will also be prevalent in what we establish. However, if there is chaos in our inner man and we are not allowing God to bring order, then what we build will likely have cracks and holes in it. This will result in the longevity of our work being temporary instead of lasting. One of the most elementary keys to building apostolically is allowing God to build in us. Just as God has created us in His direct image (Genesis 1:26), as apostolic people we have a tendency to create and build in our own image as well.

There is great wisdom in waiting on the instruction of the Lord concerning the timing of putting feet to our vision. If we try to rush a vision from the Lord, we could very well end up with a manmade movement, instead of a movement of the Spirit. We can see with the nation of Israel in 1 Samuel 8:7, that the Israelites rejected God as their king. This resulted in Saul, who was the people's king, being appointed into kingship over Israel. King Saul being appointed was a manmade movement throughout Israel, put into motion because the people couldn't wait for God's king, David, to be brought into placement by God. This restlessness that stirred within Israel caused great strain in the nation, simply because the vision that God had was put into motion too soon.

As we are being prepared by God to build for His kingdom, wisdom says to keep in step with the Spirit. We need to move forward only when He moves. We need to stay still when He is still. Whatever we build in our own strength, we will need to sustain in our own strength. However, what we build with the Lord, He sustains in His strength.

Control and False Fathering/Mothering

Apostolic leaders will often take a posture of providing accountability and governance for different individuals. This being said, they need to have a true father's or mother's heart for those who they are investing into in this capacity.

1 Corinthians 4:15: "For though you might have ten thousand instructors in Christ, yet you do not have many fathers; for in Christ Jesus I have begotten you through the gospel."

True fathers and mothers are able to get behind sons and daughters to help catapult them into their destiny. One of the most destructive pitfalls that apostolic leaders can slip into is control and false parenting. This pitfall can be so destructive because it works in complete contrast from a true apostle's mandate. An apostle is supposed to train and send out, whereas false parenting controls and suppresses.

A friend of mine once taught me something very interesting that took place in history which I believe draws a great parallel to this particular pitfall. Historically, the rulers of Egypt, pharaohs, had a terrible way of guaranteeing them authority in their reign. Since in the Old Testament kings were born into their kingship through their lineage, a pharaoh's firstborn son would one day rise into kingship. While this would often happen once the present pharaoh died, sometimes a son would challenge his father's right to reign. This is why many pharaohs in the past would at times castrate their sons, making them eunuchs as a form of control. They did this so their sons would not rise into kingship. This guaranteed that the pharaoh could remain the head of Egypt for the entirety of their lives.

I know this may seem like a gruesome example, but it parallels the effect it can have on someone if they are controlled and suppressed. If a leader walks in severe insecurity, it can spur within them a need to be seen as the most gifted, called, or anointed. This can cause them to place a manmade ceiling over emerging leaders, preventing them from rising into greatness. This form of false parenting often masquerades as "covering," yet is actually control rooted out of insecurity. I wholeheartedly believe in apostolic covering. I also wholeheartedly believe it needs to be healthy. A true apostolic ministry does not control, suppress, or micromanage; it fathers, mothers, empowers, and releases people into their full capacity. It champions people into destiny. It doesn't castrate them from rising into who they were destined to become.

Thankfully, I know many apostles and apostolic leaders who model fathering and mothering extremely well. Not only have I seen many present-day examples of this, there are also many biblical ones as well.

John the Baptist was an incredible example of one who walked in a father's heart towards those coming after him. Before Jesus' ministry began, John was the spearhead to what God was revealing to mankind. He was the talk of Israel. Look at what this great minister says in Mark 1:7: "There comes One after me who is greater than I, whose sandal strap I am not worthy to stoop down and loose."

At this time, even though John was the primary vessel for what God was doing, he would prophesy that one greater was coming whose anointing would surpass his own. He shows a true father's heart by declaring that the next generation minister would have greater impact than he did.

When Jesus arrived on the ministry scene, John even allowed one of his own disciples to follow Jesus because he knew that Jesus could bring his former disciple to a greater place of spiritual maturity than he himself could. This level of a father's heart can only take place when we come to understand that our life is about building God's kingdom instead of our own. Jesus had the same heart. He said to His disciples whom He fathered, "Most assuredly, I say to you, he who believes in Me, the works that I will do he will do also; and greater works than these he will do, because I go to My Father," (John 14:12).

King David modelled a similar heart. While David was older in years, the king's servants would bless him to comfort him by saying, "May God make the name of Solomon better than your name, and may he make his throne greater than your throne," (1 Kings 1:47). This is amazing to me. The servants didn't encourage David by telling him *his* kingdom would have a profound impact. They comforted him by telling him that his son would accomplish more than David ever could. This is a father's heart.

This is the heart every apostolic leader needs to have to see lasting fruit through their ministry. We need to believe that those who we father and mother will have greater impact and influence than we have ever dreamed of for ourselves. Whenever I speak at a church, Holy Spirit tells me to believe that every single person listening to me will go on to have a greater ministry than I myself do. He shapes a heart within me where I desire that they will see more people saved, healed, and delivered.

I truly believe God is raising up leaders who will train and equip for the sake of building God's kingdom, instead of our own. He is raising up spiritual fathers and mothers who will rejoice in seeing their children go further than they themselves do.

HOW APOSTLES FIT IN THE FIVE-FOLD

We need the entire five-fold ministry operating in unity within the church, otherwise we risk building something for God that is unbalanced. Ephesians 2:20 talks about how the household of God (the church) is built upon the foundation of the apostles and prophets. You could say, Jesus the solid rock (Matthew 7:24-27) is presented by the evangelists. Upon the solid rock, the foundation is built by the apostles and prophets. Upon the foundation, the household of God is built and shaped by pastors and teachers. We can see that if we want to build for God's kingdom with lasting significance, then we need to see the fullness of God's leadership not only in action, but functioning in unity.

With every five-fold office there are strengths as well as blind spots. This is why God has called the five-fold ministry to work together as a team, instead of independently. In this chapter, I would like to shed light concerning how some of these different offices can work together with the apostolic office, how they complement one another, and what tensions may exist between them.

Apostles and Prophets

Ephesians 2:19-20: "Now, therefore, you are no longer strangers and foreigners, but fellow citizens with the saints and members of the household of God, having been built on the foundation of the apostles and prophets, Jesus Christ Himself being the chief cornerstone."

The apostolic and prophetic offices are a match made in heaven. When Paul the apostle would make a statement such as this saying that the household of God is built upon the foundation of the apostles and prophets, he didn't draw such conclusions simply through his experience. Paul was a theologian, and he understood that much of what was recorded in the Old Testament was a foreshadow of what Jesus would do in New Testament times. We can actually see strong parallels in how apostles and prophets would build together through how kings and prophets partnered with one another in the Old Testament.

The kings of Israel in many ways operated similar to how apostles function within the church today. This is true in the sense that kings in the Old Testament were the ones who provided the vision, governance, covering, and order to the culture of Israel, just as apostles do for the church. Just as kings and prophets co-laboured together to build foundations for Israel, so will apostles and prophets for the church.

In the Old Testament, prophets prophetically advised the king whom they served. This means they heard from God for those who He called to lead a nation. While the king received the initial vision for Israel, the prophet would then bring guidance by the word of the Lord in how that vision should be established. The same should be for apostles and prophets today. You could say that apostles receive the vision in God's heart concerning what to build for God's kingdom, and the prophet guides the apostle's hand as he or she builds.

I have seen many apostles try to build vision that God has given them without prophetic guidance. This usually leaves many blind spots in the structure of what is being established, because prophetic discernment is not keeping what is being built within the direct will of the Lord. Apostles often possess the gifts required to build for God's kingdom that prophets do not; yet prophets carry the ability to hear the Lord so the building can be done properly. God has created apostles and prophets to have a kingdom dependency upon one another.

Proverbs 29:18: "Where there is no vision, the people perish."

If you were to translate the word "vision" from Hebrew, this word literally means "prophetic vision." In spite of his fall in later years, king Solomon, the author of Proverbs was one of the most accomplished apostolic leaders in the Old Testament. What he wrote in this verse shows us that as an apostolic leader, he understood that ordinary vision was not enough to prevent people from perishing. They needed prophetic vision straight from the heart of God. King Solomon had a revelation of the importance in receiving from prophets to acquire prophetic direction and insight.

If a prophetic leader receives insight concerning vision and guidance for an apostolic leader, they need to understand what they are accountable for. As a prophetic person, if we receive this form of word for leadership, it is our job to take it to the Lord in prayer and to properly judge it, making sure it falls in line with proper prophetic etiquette. Once we do this and deliver the word, our job is done. Some prophetic people take on a false burden by trying to make their words come to pass. They try to control the leadership into the direction they feel things should go. This is manipulation, so we shouldn't have any part in this. The prophetic and apostolic relationship operates out of honour by respecting one another's capacity to lead in their entrusted office.

Remember the example of Paul and Agabus in Acts 21. Agabus warns Paul through a prophetic word, and Paul chose to go ahead with what he felt the Lord told him to do. Agabus didn't try to force Paul into doing what he thought he should do. He did his part as a prophet by judging the word, delivering it, and honouring Paul as an apostle.

We can see how an apostle's vision can falter without the help of a prophet, yet this partnership is two-sided. Apostles benefit prophets by showing them where and how they fit within in greater picture of God's plans. I have met far too many prophetic people who are lone-rangers, who try to single handedly advance God's kingdom. We were not created to build God's kingdom alone, but together with one another. Apostles carry the ability to make room for every type of ministry in the church, including the ministry of the prophetic and the office of a prophet.

We can see a very clear partnership of an apostle and prophet co-labouring together in New Testament times. We often overlook this, but Jesus and John the Baptist co-laboured together as an apostle and prophet throughout Israel. Jesus came as an apostle to present His vision given by the Father, which was that the kingdom of heaven would be established on the earth. John the Baptist's job as a prophet was to make straight the way of the Lord, so Jesus' apostolic vision could be established.

As an apostle and prophet, we can even see how Jesus and John the Baptist co-laboured that they could lay a proper foundation for us (Ephesians 2:20). 1 Corinthians 3:11 says, "For no other foundation can anyone lay than that which is laid, which is Jesus Christ."

Jesus the great Apostle laid himself down as the foundation for us to build the kingdom of heaven upon. John the Baptist did foundational work with Jesus as a prophet by making sure that every valley would be filled, and every mountain and hill brought low (Luke 3:5). John as a prophet prepared the way for Jesus, so that as our Great Foundation, He could properly lay upon a level land throughout Israel. This solid foundation that was laid by Jesus and John the Baptist, as an apostle and prophet, is the foundation that everything we now build for the kingdom is established upon.

Apostles and Evangelists

It is crucial that apostles and evangelists work together, even though there can often be tension in this ministerial relationship. This tension often lies within apostles not understanding the function of an evangelist and evangelists fearing being controlled.

Evangelists carry a reputation for being the wild-child of the five-fold ministry; however, this is not a poor quality. Evangelists are the ones who are called to help make the church mobile. A part of their gift to the church is to be wild and out of the box. When apostles do not understand an evangelist's role within the five-fold ministry, they could slip into a mentality of trying to control an evangelist's expression. This often results in evangelists trying to minister independently from the local church, taking an independent stance in ministry instead of a unified one. Health is brought to this relationship when the apostolic functions from this principle: a true apostolic ministry does not control, it sends out.

We can see a brilliant example of apostles and evangelists working together in Acts 8. Phillip the evangelist was sent out to go before the apostles to a territory where knowledge of the Lord was scarce. He would minister in miracles, signs, and wonders, thus seeing mass salvations. We can then see that the apostles would follow up with the ministry that Phillip would do. The apostles would go to bring stability to what Phillip birthed, so that it could last with longevity. Phillip would spark the first flame, and the apostles would make sure the flame did not die out by bringing order to the movement. Apostles made sure that the evangelist's spark would become a wildfire for kingdom advancement.

As apostles understand the role of evangelists and learn to healthily release them, we begin to see the kingdom of God stretching beyond the four walls of the church. Evangelists actually benefit apostles by expanding apostolic vision to wherever they preach the gospel. Evangelists also help apostles in remembering that their grand vision needs to always point towards reaching those who do not yet know Jesus.

Evangelists can often struggle with understanding their placement within the local church. This is where apostles can greatly benefit evangelists. Since apostles carry a grace to understand the big picture of God's kingdom, they can lead evangelists to understand where they fit within the body of Christ. It is in this place of partnership, accountability, and relationship where we can see these two ministries function at a more complete capacity.

Apostles and Pastors

There has been an unfortunate lack of apostles and pastors working together. This is often due to the fact that we have in many ways laid the apostolic office to the wayside, and have expected pastors to pick up the mandate of governance in churches and ministries. Biblically, we can see the Jesus rose up apostles to take a role of governance in the church. This is why he invested into and commissioned the twelve apostles, not the twelve pastors.

A pastor's realm of authority in training the church is in the soul and in relationships. Since this is the case, there is something very interesting that occurs when we have pastoral oversight instead of apostolic governance in churches or ministries. Since pastors are in many ways internally focused, we have very internally focused churches. We end up with ministries that have very healthy people emotionally, socially, and relationally; however, we easily forget about the grander mission of the kingdom of heaven invading earth. Extreme pastoral cultures that do not have an apostolic revelation will often step into a posture that isolates the church from having a grand kingdom impact in society.

Apostles have a revelation of the grander mission of the kingdom of heaven. Apostles bring great balance to pastors because they don't only think about internal health, but also outward impact. An apostle's mandate is to train the church how to advance God's kingdom in every person's sphere of influence. This is why pastors function more healthily under apostolic accountability, compared to apostles submitting to pastoral headship. In God's biblical order, an apostolic leader would be providing governance so that the vision of a church or ministry can remain on track with the will of God. In this place, pastors can shepherd individuals into freedom, wholeness, and in how to walk in relationships so we can have healthy people advancing God's kingdom everywhere they go.

Apostles and Teachers

1 Corinthians 12:28: "And God has appointed these in the church: first apostles, second prophets, third teachers, after that miracles, then gifts of healings, helps, administrations, varieties of tongues."

Apostles and teachers are called to co-labour together in a very interesting way. In 1 Corinthians 12:28, there is an interesting order that Paul uses while listing who God has appointed in the church. God appoints, first apostles, second prophets, and third teachers. Apostles and prophets, God's first and second appointed, are often focused on bridging heaven to earth. When this happens, revival atmosphere is created; the supernatural occurs. God thirdly appoints the teacher, which is crucial if we are to see healthy kingdom culture. While apostles and prophets help bridge heaven to earth, teachers will play a role of training the church to understand how the move of the Spirit is both biblical and from the heart of God. While apostles and prophets are focused on what God is doing, teachers are focused on how people are responding to what God is doing. Teachers have the ability to biblically, practically, and intellectually unpack what is happening in the supernatural realm. This way, everyone is able to comprehend what the Lord is doing.

I have seen times when the Lord is pouring out supernaturally through either an apostolic or prophetic leader in a church meeting; however, what the Lord was doing wasn't received by a large amount of people in the service. This was actually because there was no one there with a teaching anointing to articulate properly was taking place. Teachers partnering with apostolic leaders helps demystify the things of the Spirit, so they become accessible and comprehendible to everyone.

Teachers can also benefit apostles by helping communicate the apostolic vision to the people they are called to lead. Sometimes since apostles have vision for the masses, they have troubles communicating to the individual. This is where teachers can come in. Teachers can help an apostle not only to communicate their vision, but also to explain to the people how they fit into the grander vision as individuals.

APOSTOLIC PRAYER

If you have a heart to grow in your relationship with Jesus the Apostle, pray this prayer with me:

"Jesus, I receive You as my Apostle. Thank you for the sphere of influence You have given me. Teach me to steward it with love, integrity, and excellence. Teach me to see what burns in Your heart concerning what You've entrusted to me. Help me to see the blueprint for my life. Give me eyes to see clearly and hands that build with wisdom and excellence. I pray that You bring the right apostolic voices in my life to help me in what I'm called to build. On earth as it is in heaven in my places of mandate. I pray this in Jesus' name."

OFFICE OF A
PROPHET

The world tries to barricade our identity brick by brick, to mask who we truly are with cold and calloused stone. As prophetic people, we are called to fix our perspective to see through the eyes of God. We are called to see past dysfunction into the vast fortress of undiscovered treasure. Prophecy sees through stone and calls forth castled destinies.

DEFINING A PROPHET

There is a lot of mysticism and misunderstanding surrounding the term "prophet." For those of us who don't have experience with the prophetic ministry, our perception of what a prophet is would likely be greatly skewed. In fact, if we were to try to imagine a prophet, we might conjure up an image of a hermit in the wilderness who is highly mystical and lacks social skills. However, this stereotype couldn't be further from the truth.

Prophets in the Old Testament were counsellors to kings and the keepers of God's word. To hold such a position, prophets would have been those who stood for truth and holiness from a place of unwavering integrity. Just as God has risen up prophets pre-cross, He is raising them up in present times. The prophets who I personally know, God is using throughout the earth to bring profound healing to the nations. They do this while standing in Godly character and integrity, in friendship with the Lord.

Something very important for us to comprehend while understanding what a prophet is, is the difference between prophets and prophetic people. Often, due to a lack of definition, we have a tendency to assume that they are the same thing, when really they are distinctly different.

Back in the 1980's when there was a wave of restoration concerning the prophetic ministry, it was commonly believed that if you prophesied, you were a prophet. This resulted in many people self-proclaiming themselves as prophets and prophetesses of God. We need to understand that while scripture tells us that every believer can prophesy, not everyone who prophesies is a prophet. We are all called to prophesy; however, to be a prophet is a very set apart calling from the Lord.

We can see in the Old Testament that there were many people who prophesied, yet were not prophets. King Saul was a great example of this. In 1 Samuel 10, Saul encountered a concession of prophets. Since He was with them, he began to prophesy alongside with them. It is important to note that even though Saul prophesied, he is not scripturally referred to as a prophet. This shows us that there is much more responsibility required to being a prophet than simply prophesying.

Those who have the calling of a true prophet are God-appointed and people-appointed; never self-appointed. Don't worry, I will unpack that statement for you. I believe that every prophet is called by God through some sort of encounter with Him. Prophets in the Bible were not called and risen up by man; they were first and foremost called and risen up by God. We can see this with how God first called the prophet Jeremiah.

Jeremiah 1:5: "Before I formed you in the womb I knew you; before you were born I sanctified you; I ordained you a prophet to the nations."

Prophets aren't only God-appointed; they are people-appointed. If you are a prophet, you shouldn't have to run around calling yourself one to be recognized as such. In fact, as you live out the unique expression of the calling, leaders should begin to recognize the mantle over your life. Prophets are people-appointed in the sense that credible leaders should recognize the calling, without us having to self-identify ourselves.

Having a prophetic ministry, I meet many who self-proclaim themselves as prophets. I am often very leery of those who do this. If you are publicly calling yourself a prophet, you should be able to show the fruit of a prophet, which is spiritual sons and daughters who prophesy and trust with influential leaders who allow you to speak the word of the Lord to their lives. Even for those who do walk in the office of a prophet, I believe it's only wise to refer to yourself as one if the Lord permits you.

I myself am recognized as a prophetic leader in the church throughout the nations; yet to date, I've never once called myself a prophet for two reasons: Firstly, the Lord hasn't released me to do so. Secondly, I've always been one to believe that humility opens more doors than self-promotion does.

Prophets weren't only for Old Testament times. Based on my experience and what I can see biblically, I believe we can see three primary characteristics that mark someone who truly walks in the office of a prophet:

Prophets Teach how to Hear the Voice of God

The prophet Samuel shows us an excellent example of a true prophet. 1 Samuel 3:1 tells us that when Samuel the prophet was called by God, in those days the word of the Lord was rare in Israel. Samuel did far more than prophesy; he was a gift to Israel, mandated to make God's word common again. Not only did Samuel prophesy to common-day people, but he appointed kings by the direction of God. Samuel was a prophetic counsellor and advisor to both kings and priests. He even rose up a concession of prophets who he seemingly trained himself (1 Samuel 10). In Samuel, God rose up one man who made the word of the Lord common throughout an entire nation. We can actually see the fruit of Samuel's ministry echoing throughout generations in 1 Kings and 2 Kings, with the vast amount of prophets who were risen up in that time. These prophets were likely the fruit from Samuel's ability to train and equip others to walk in the prophetic office.

This is the function of prophets today. Their function is not only to prophesy; it is to live in a time where the word of the Lord is seemingly rare, and to make it common again.

Prophets play an important role in the church to hear and declare God's word; however, a key function of the prophetic office is to train and equip the church to do what comes natural to a prophet. This is one of the characteristics that separates a prophet from prophetic people. Prophetic people prophesy; whereas prophets not only prophesy, they train people how to do it as well.

Since prophets have a grace over their lives to see and hear what God is doing, their function in ministry is to equip others to do the same. This means prophets are ordained by God to demystify things such as the still small quiet voice of God, visions, dreams, angelic visitations, and prophetic encounters showing their accessibility to all believers. Someone who has a prophetic gift, their words are a gift to the body of Christ; whereas a prophet himself/herself is God's gift to His church to make the word of the Lord common amongst His people.

Jesus said something very interesting in Matthew 10:41, "Whoever welcomes a prophet as a prophet will receive a prophet's reward." What is the prophet's reward, you ask? A prophet's reward is to see what the Lord is doing and to hear what the Lord is saying. Receiving the ministry of prophets results in the body of Christ's ears awakening to the voice of God.

One of my greatest joys is getting to train others how to hear the voice of God. Through travelling and speaking, I've had the honour of training thousands to hear God and speak His word. In ministry schools where I teach on the prophetic ministry, we have people who at first don't even believe God wants to speak to them. They struggle with hearing even the faintest of words from His lips. Yet as the school progresses, His voice becomes more clear. By the end, these very students are able to give a dozen prophetic words, one after another. How exciting! This takes place because in my life, I've cultivated a lifestyle where I'm constantly positioned to hear God's voice. Therefore, when students sit under my ministry they aren't only listening to me teach, they are being engulfed by the atmosphere of my internal culture. They are getting a taste of my "daily bread" per-say.

The most exciting part of this for me is when students take what they've learned into their specific circles of life. I love hearing stories of mothers prophesying and speaking life into their children. I love hearing about evangelistic people giving prophetic words to people in coffee shops, or of business owners asking the Lord for prophetic strategies for growth. God's heart is for multiplication, that His word won't be rare, but common throughout the earth. Embracing the ministry of prophets is a prominent key in seeing this come to pass.

Prophets Keep the Prophetic Ministry Pure

Unfortunately to say the prophetic ministry has always been utilized properly, wouldn't be a truthful statement. While we are now seeing purity in this ministry, it hasn't always been this way. Several years ago when there was a restoration of the prophetic ministry, it breaks my heart to say that many were hurt due to a lack of understanding concerning prophecy. These were times when everyone thought prophesying was all about correction, judgement, doom, and gloom. I'll quickly share with you why I believe we slipped into such misconceptions of prophecy.

In 1988, as the global church, we experienced a swift acceleration of understanding concerning our accessibility to the voice of the Lord through the cross.

As people who are under the New Covenant, we examined the New Testament, looking for a prophetic leader to see how we should prophesy. Quickly, the emerging prophetic community discovered that there is not a vast amount of New Testament prophets in the Bible to study. In fact, the variety of those who were actually called prophets, other than Jesus, is minimal leaving us with only Agabus (Acts 21:10), Judas and Silas (Acts 15:32), of which there is very little mentioning. Since we didn't see an embodiment of a prophetic figure after the cross and resurrection, we unfortunately dismissed Paul's teachings concerning this particular ministry in 1 Corinthians 14.

We had a hungry group of people wanting to learn how to hear God's voice and speak His word. Since we didn't see many prophets to refer to in the New Testament, the body of Christ looked where there was a vast variety of prophets; in the Old Testament.

The church began to use the Old Testament prophets as a template of how to prophesy. Now, what happened when we did this, is that as New Testament people, we stepped into an Old Covenant mindset and began to prophesy under Old Testament principals. A primary function of a prophet's job in the Old Testament was to point out people's sin, since Jesus hadn't yet died on the cross yet; therefore, sin stood as a barrier between man and God. A bulk of their ministry was geared towards bringing correction, in hope that the people would repent and eliminate the sin in their lives that there may be reconciliation between man and God. If the people didn't repent, it was then often a prophet's job to declare the repercussions of their stubbornness through condemnation and judgement. Since this was a common trait in Old Testament prophecy, many people in 1988 began to prophesy from the standpoint of condemnation and judgement.

You can imagine how many people would have been hurt by this form of ministry. This is when it became popular for ministers to prophetically point-out people's sin publicly in church meetings, which I never agree with or condone in any way. I do not believe it is ever God's heart to humiliate His children. Since so many people were hurt by prophecy in the 80's, many rejected it completely. Ever since this point in history, many in the church have been in a process of healing based on what happened due to misconceptions concerning prophecy.

I believe what Paul wrote in 1 Corinthians 14:3 is an excellent template for New Testament prophecy. It says, "He who prophesies speaks edification and exhortation and comfort to men."

While Old Testament prophecy brought judgement and condemnation, New Testament prophecy brings 'edification' which means to build up, 'exhortation' which means to encourage, and comfort. We need to understand that the expression of prophecy has shifted because the covenant we live under has changed.

In the present, mature prophets have been righting the wrongs of the past by working to create proper boundaries surrounding prophecy, so it can be a safe ministry to function in. Myself, as well as many others have working with leaders, churches, and ministries all around the world, helping to restore health to this extremely important ministry.

One of the things I'm most passionate about is bringing purity back to the prophetic ministry. Operating in more of a prophetic capacity, you would think I would primarily speak to Charismatic and Pentecostal groups. However, thankfully I've also had the honour of ministering to those who are far more conservative in their faith. On many occasions, I'll be speaking to a conservative group, and right when I say the word "prophecy," I can feel the room light up in anxiety and fear. It's amazing how a gift of the Spirit has become a trigger-word for many, simply due to misuse of the gift. I then get to explain about the heart of prophecy, which directly reflects the heart of our loving Father in heaven. After teaching and walking them through exercises in hearing the voice of God, I get to watch people's fears fade as they begin to catch

God's heart. Thankfully, I've seen countless people, leaders, and churches who once feared the prophetic ministry, change their thinking to once again embrace Jesus as Prophet.

Prophets Advise

While we are all called to prophesy, the audience that a prophetic person might speak to compared to a prophet can be quite different. Prophetic people might prophesy over their family members, co-workers, or people at the grocery store; while a prophet will be entrusted to speak the word of the Lord to highly influential people.

In Old Testament times, prophets didn't only speak the word of God to the common Israelite. Many prophets were counsellors of kings. They gave strategy for war. They were the ones who were initially entrusted to make people aware of the coming of Christ, which was a tremendously important task. The same is of the prophets God is raising up today. God is raising up prophetic mouth pieces to bring Spirit-led encouragement and direction to those who have influence not only in the church, but also in the world. I personally know several prophets who speak the word of the Lord into world leaders.

In my personal ministry, I have different sides to what I do. I have the front end of my ministry that is extremely public, which involves public speaking and being an author. However, I also have a very private part of my ministry which consists of me speaking prophetically into leaders. My wife can attest to how often I'm downstairs in my office on the phone speaking into the lives of people who are government leaders, CEO's, apostolic leaders, or celebrities. I have the honour of getting to wait on the Lord and to share God's message with them. That being said, I've needed to allow my ears to become attuned to His voice. This doesn't happen overnight. It's taken years for the Lord to refine my ability to hear Him, so I could be entrusted to speak to such influential people. I make it a constant exercise to try to be tapped into what He's saying.

The prophet Isaiah had great understanding of the prophetic office and I believe he said it best:

Isaiah 50:4: "The Sovereign LORD has given me a well-instructed tongue, to know the word that sustains the weary. He wakens me morning by morning, wakens my ear to listen like one being instructed."

While I've had much experience with giving more common prophetic words, prophetically advising those in high places of influence is quite different. In chatting with prophets I know, I've recognized that there is a common trait that the Lord tends to focus on shaping within them. He trains them in the fear of the Lord, in the context of friendship with Him.

Amos 3:7: "Surely the Lord God does nothing, unless He reveals His secret to His servants the prophets."

God has no obligation to share His secrets with prophets. Yet, He shares His secrets with the prophets because they are His friends, and because they've learned to value the weight of His words. When a true prophet speaks into the ears of the influential, their words can encourage kings, reform culture, and change nations.

COMMON PITFALLS OF THE PROPHETIC

The prophetic ministry is an irreplaceable part of God's kingdom. However, if we are going to see it utilized to its full expression, we need to be aware of its potential pitfalls. Just like every ministry, it is beneficial when it is healthy, however it can also cause hurt and pain if it's not wielded with love and integrity. Since I have much experience training people in the prophetic ministry, I have become quite familiar with understanding the pitfalls that can follow prophets and highly prophetic people.

Here are some pitfalls that can be experienced by prophets and those who are highly prophetic:

Dismissing the Practical

Highly prophetic people will often have a tendency to naturally excel in things that are spiritual. Since there is such a grace to tap into things of the Spirit, there can often be a lack of understanding of the importance of things that are more practical. This will often result in us being tremendously gifted, yet we could have very noticeable holes in our life-skills.

I will share something with you: before I was in full time ministry, I thought that in order to have a legitimate ministry all I would need to do is know how to teach well, know how to prophesy accurately, and have enough faith to see the sick healed. When I did start up my ministry, I was blown away by how practically you need to think in order to run something such as a ministry with excellence. I quickly began to understand that even if I can move in the gifts of the Spirit, if I do not have a focus on administration then I will not be able to impact as many people as I would like to with these gifts.

There is a side to moving in the Spirit which is completely supernatural, yet there is another side that is tremendously practical as well. I need to know how to prophesy, as well as know how to keep on top of bookings for speaking engagements. I need to know how to pray for the sick, as well as know how to have good enough people skills to come across well when interacting with other leaders throughout the world. If I were not willing to continually grow in my faith for the supernatural, as well as in my life-skills, I could be giving the enemy an access-point to dim the impact I have through my life.

It is not false humility to acknowledge our weaknesses and areas that we need to grow in. As for myself, I've found tremendous value in acknowledging that one of my weaknesses as an individual is practicality. This is not everyone's weakness. However, I know that it is not something I naturally excel in. In recognizing this in myself, I've had the opportunity to surround myself with people who could coach me in more practical ways. For example, I surround myself with different business leaders to help give counsel and insight as to how I should run the practical side of my ministry. I needed to learn that even though practicality is not an area I naturally thrive in, this is not an excuse for me to not develop skills that will benefit my life and size of impact I'm called to have.

Whether it is our health, finances, relationships, or any other aspect of life, we need to understand how the supernatural and the practical are supposed to blend together in us. I would go as far as to say that in order to walk in a place of maturity as a spiritual person, we need to be a place where both the supernatural and the practical marry.

Over-Spiritualizing Assumption

Something I've often observed while working with many different prophetic groups, is many will have the tendency to slip into the tyranny of assumption. What I mean by this is that those of us who are highly prophetic can develop a bad habit of trusting our discernment more than those who we are in trusted relationships with. I will paint a picture for you:

Say that you are in close relationship with someone. We will call her Betty. You have known Betty for a few years now and have spent much time with her. One day at church, you see Betty and as you are crossing paths, it almost seems as though she is trying to avoid eye contact with you. This is highly unlike her, considering you two connect very well. All of a sudden, you're left feeling confused. Soon after, you find yourself frantically searching through your memory, trying to see if you can think of what you may have done to offend her. Suddenly, you feel your confusion concerning the situation switching to frustration towards her. This leads your mind to begin to assume what Betty is feeling towards you, which can lead anyone down a scary road when assumption is in control of the wheel.

When there is a lack of training on kingdom relationships in a prophetic community, things can go south very quickly. Someone who doesn't know how to wield their discernment gift with maturity may begin to assume things about the person who they are in conflict with, which are in fact not true. In their hurt, based on what they are assuming, they then can easily label that assumption as "discernment". All of a sudden, there is a clear wedge within a relationship simply because we do not know how to do healthy communication.

For those who have revelation concerning how to do healthy conflict, the obvious solution would have been to approach Betty, asking her if something is wrong for the sake of not allowing assumption to swell. However, for those who may be highly gifted prophetically, we can have a tendency to have more trust in our gifting, rather than in our ability to talk things through in relationships.

Often when we are in an emotional situation, such as having to do with relationships, our emotions can cloud our discernment. If we are only depending on our discernment in a situation such as this, then in the name of "discernment" we can then easily begin to build a case towards someone. We could be creating unnecessary distance with them, simply because we are not willing to do healthy communication. This could then even result in us talking badly about this person to others, which begins stepping into the territory of gossip and slander.

It is of utmost importance that those who are primarily geared towards gifts of discernment receive proper pastoral training in how to do relationships healthily. If a discerning person struggles with insecurity, they may think they are discerning other people's offenses towards them. This will often create a void of assumption where the enemy can speak lies. Discerning people need to learn how to do healthy conflict and communication to disarm offense which may be made up.

Probably some of the best advice I can give an emerging leader is this: leading people is messy.

Walking in relationship with people is messy. Instead of assuming other's faults and complaining about the mess, we need to learn how to grab a mop and clean it up. We need to learn how to do conflict and communication well in our relationships if we ever want to be part of a team. Instead of only depending on our gifts, we need to allow God to develop our people skills in our relationships. Discernment and assumption are two different things entirely, so we cannot merge them. Discernment is when God gives us insight into a situation; whereas assumption is making an intellectual and emotional analysis, which could easily be tainted by whatever is occurring within our soul.

Gnosticism

In the last decade or so, there has been a vast amount of revelation hitting the church concerning prophetic experiences. God has been revealing to the church the accessibility and invitation that we have to different experiences and encounters men and women of God have had in biblical times. These are things that we have an access to through the cross.

Some of these encounters God has been shining light on include: transportation (Acts 8:26-40), angelic visitations (Matthew 4:11), third-heaven encounters (Isaiah 6, Ezekiel 1, Daniel 7), and visitations from the Lord Himself (Acts 9:1-19). Prophetic encounters are along the mystical side of the prophetic ministry. Many try to steer away from this realm of Christianity, even though prophetic encounters with God can be a pivotal tool to wholeness and Christlikeness.

Some elements of prophetic encounters can come across as weird; however, I believe that a more appropriate way to describe them would be to say that it is supernatural. Supernatural things have a tendency to offend our minds because it stretches beyond the laws of the natural. As intellectuals, we can have a tendency to dismiss whatever does not fit into our intellectual grid. That being said, we need to learn to be a people who do not fix our eyes on what is seen, but rather on what is unseen (2 Corinthians 4:18).

Just like many revelations that the church receives, there are those who take these new truths to unhealthy extremes. This is where we can step into some pitfalls with prophetic encounters. I am an advocate for prophetic experiences; however, such things need to be sourced by love and stewarded with integrity. I know many highly prophetic people where such experiences are very common because there is a grace for them to experience God in such a way. If there is a grace to see and hear the word of the Lord in a more mystical way, yet we are not rooted in love and grounded in Godly character, there can often be a pull towards forms of Gnosticism.

Gnosticism was a belief back in biblical times that taught against Jesus' divinity, and pushed people into the worship of man's spirit. Gnosticism led people in the direction of dismissing the importance of anything of the natural realm, only seeing value with things that are potently spiritual or mystical.

I have met many who have diligently pursued prophetic encounters, yet were not rooted in relationship with the Lord. What this did was it caused them to transition from a place of deeming prophetic encounters as a tool to know the Lord more, into believing that an encounter was the end goal. If our goal in desiring prophetic encounters is not to know the Lord more in friendship, then we are likely doing it out of an unhealthy curiosity of the supernatural, or out of an insecurity to be deemed as spiritual. Pursuing such experiences with a poor heart posture can open up many doors for deception such as a worship of spiritual experiences, Gnosticism, and even New Age mentalities.

If our heart posture is incorrect while desiring such encounters, we could end up being led by our own will rather than by Holy Spirit. I'm very open to prophetic encounters. I want whatever the Lord wants for me; however, if Holy Spirit isn't in control of the wheel, I don't want anything to do with it.

Not only should we be rooted in a hunger to know the Lord more if we are desiring such experiences, but we should also be rooted in the written word of God, the Bible. Every day I am blown away by the depth of scripture. It is such an amazing tool that God has given us to understand His heart and character. When pursuing prophetic encounters, relationship with Holy Spirit and being rooted in the Bible is what keeps us grounded in truth. I have seen many people go off the deep-end in what they perceive is truth because they see more validity in what they have felt prophetically, compared to what is written in scripture. As a result, their doctrine is 90% rooted in encounter, and only 10% rooted in the Bible. We always need to remember that the prophetic word will always submit to the written word. Every time. Everything we experience prophetically may not be written in black and white in the Bible, but scripture should always support what we experience. The prophetic should never contradict scripture because God's word is not divided.

Prophetic encounters are a tool to encounter the love of God. What they should do is infuse us with love so we can love those around us better. In the scriptural accounts of prophetic encounters throughout the Bible, there was a natural manifestation from such experiences. This means that you can test the validity of the encounter by the tangibility of its fruit. Ezekiel's heavenly encounter in Ezekiel 1 resulted in him stepping into his prophetic calling to bring change to Israel. Paul the apostle's encounter when Jesus came to him in Acts 9, launched him into understanding the cross so he could be an apostle to the nations.

It is fine to pursue supernatural encounters; however, we need to do it from a place of hunger to encounter the love of God. This should result in us loving those around us better. If someone is having these types of encounters, yet they are not radiating more love as the byproduct, then I believe we have the right to question the legitimacy of the encounter.

Rejection and Isolation

One of the most common pitfalls with highly prophetic people and prophets is isolation. The reason being is that many highly gifted prophetic people hear from the Lord in a way that may seem uncommon. If they are in circles where the things of the Spirit are not embraced, this could bring much rejection due to people's lack of understanding of the prophetic ministry. I have met many highly prophetic people who have experienced heart breaking rejection from the church. In my earlier years, I myself have gone through much rejection from the church, due to the call that is over my life and the uniqueness of my relationship with the Lord. That being said, in order for a prophetic person to cultivate a healthy prophetic lifestyle, we need to be woven into relationship within the family of God. One of the quickest ways to fall into deception as a prophetic person is by stepping out of community.

Time and time again I have met prophetic people who because of wounding try to avoid being accountable in relationships. Often prophetic people will interpret the freedom that the cross granted us as freedom from commitment. We can slip into a lie which assumes that our gift works better apart from covering and accountability because it feels more free. If you are reading this and you fall into this category, I will tell you first hand: trying to operate as a prophetic person apart from community and accountability will lead you down a long road of wounding. Freedom and liberty is not anarchy, it is being able to come under proper fathering and mothering, to function as part of a family and to serve the way Jesus did. The only way you will be able to reach your full potential as a prophetic person is by being around others who can build into your weak areas. By yourself, you will have clear blind spots; whereas in community those with different personalities and ministries will begin to form Jesus in the areas where you lack. That being said, while there may be people around us who we face rejection from, every one of us should also be surrounding ourselves with people who receive us as we are, who we can walk in relationship with.

If we choose to be separate from the body of Christ due to fear of rejection, we are in many ways stealing the prophetic ministry from the church. We need to find apostolic accountability instead of attempting to adopt principles and a heart posture of individualism.

The church needs the prophetic ministry as much as prophetic people need the body of Christ. The prophetic ministry reconciles the church as a family by revealing the body's diversity in all of its callings, mantels, anointings, giftings, and talents. Prophecy actually shows the church that it cannot function properly if it's fragmented, and that every aspect of God through His people has precious value.

If you are reading this and you have felt rejection from the church because of your prophetic calling, as a leader in the church, and on behalf of the church, I apologize to you. I declare over you that you are irreplaceable in the heart of God, and valuable in the kingdom of heaven. There is a place in the family of God that fits who you are perfectly. You were not created to walk alone. You were created to know that you belong. I pray that Jesus surrounds you with those who will both accept and love you; I pray that fathers and mothers of the faith will come around you to help you steward and nurture your gifts and calling.

Manipulation and Control

Extreme pride and control can be some of the more dangerous pitfalls to those who are highly prophetic. The reason why is that these pitfalls do not only hurt the person operating in them, but they could end up wounding many people. When prophetic people have slipped into a deep wound of rejection from the church, it can be easy for them to believe that the entire church is in rebellion towards God. This can spark a significant spiritual pride in someone, considering they are believing the whole church is in the wrong, and they themselves are in the right. While it is true that none of us has a full revelation of who God is, to assume that we have the right to blatantly and bluntly call out rebellion in church leaders, that is a very presumptuous assumption to make. We should be leaving such judgements to God. For those who have embraced such deep wounds to assume that the entire church is in rebellion, I have seen the enemy take a few individuals down a road of much greater deception. Out of a place of pride, they would try to operate in prophetic giftings towards the church from a place of tremendous wounding and bitterness. This would result in them manipulating and controlling others with their prophetic gift.

Matthew 7:15-16: "Beware of false prophets, who come to you in sheep's clothing, but inwardly they are ravenous wolves. You will know them by their fruits."

The difference between true prophets as opposed to false prophets, is that true prophets point to Jesus, whereas false prophets point to themselves. When I use the term "false prophet" I am not referring to someone who has given an incorrect prophetic word, because we are all learning and growing in how we hear the Lord. I am referring to those who out of pride use their prophetic gifting to intentionally manipulate and control others because they are wounded. I honestly do not throw the term "false prophet" around much at all, and when I do, I am very careful in doing so. In fact, in my years of ministry I have met very few people who I believe walk in this level of deception. However, we need to be aware of the schemes of the enemy through false prophets. We also need to be testing our own hearts to make sure that we are ministering from a place of love, instead of out of soulish desires.

False prophets minister out of a place of wounding and insecurity. Since they are hurt, they will often use their gift as means for attention and to manipulate. Something I have seen being a common characteristic of false prophets, is that they have a tendency to come into churches, and use their gift as a way to trick vulnerable church members into believing that the leadership is in rebellion. The false prophet will then try to take a place of leadership over those whom they have deceived. This of course brings division within churches. False prophets are very manipulation driven and have a reputation of twisting the scriptures to lure people into their self-promoting theologies and doctrines.

Those who walk in this level of deception have often been hurt by the church, so therefore walk in a lone-ranger mentality. Someone who is walking in maturity in the office of a prophet will not do so independently from the church, just as prophets in the Old Testament did not function as prophets apart from Israel. That being said, if someone isn't recognized as a prophet in a church, they can't try to walk in authority that hasn't been given by leadership. Prophets are supposed to function alongside of those in authority, not against them. Even if you are a well-known prophet throughout the nations, when you come into a local church to minister, you need to submit to the local authorities.

Pastors, beware of false prophets. If one tries to operate in your church, do not be intimidated by them. Do not be swayed by impressive gifting if their character does not add up. If they are turning people away from Jesus and attempting to dethrone you as a leader, do what is necessary to protect those who God has entrusted to you.

False prophets will often live their lives from a Messiah complex, tricking people into believing that they are the only ones who carry the authority to bring freedom to others. Matthew 7:16 says, "You will know them by their fruit." A false prophet's fruit will be a trail of broken people who are dependent upon them; whereas a true prophet's fruit will be sons and daughters who build up the church through the prophetic ministry.

God has called His true prophets and prophetesses to be fathers and mothers in the church. Many prophets in the Old Testament carried a reputation of being borderline militant. Moses stands in contrast to many of the other prophets in the Old Testament. Moses was not just a prophet to Israel, he was also a father and pastor to Israel. Deuteronomy 9 tells of when Moses was on Mount Sinai receiving the commandments of God, when God spoke to Moses telling him that the Israelites had sinned against Him. God spoke to Moses in Deuteronomy 9:14 and said, "Let Me alone, that I may destroy them and blot out their name from under heaven; and I will make of you a nation mightier and greater than they."

In this verse, I personally believe God was testing Moses' heart as a leader. Out of a desire to have a great name, Moses could have taken this offer to be a great nation, yet since he loved the Israelites he laid facedown for fourty days and fourty nights fasting and interceding for Israel that God would reconsider. The mark of a mature prophet is the ability to lay down their life for the church out of love.

Ephesians 2:19-20: "Now, therefore, you are no longer strangers and foreigners, but fellow citizens with the saints and members of the household of God, having been built on the foundation of the apostles and prophets, Jesus Christ Himself being the chief cornerstone."

To be a prophet is not to lord over people. It is not to manipulate or control out of pride. It is to become the greatest servant. It is not a ministry where you stand above everyone; it is foundational. You take the posture of a servant to all, believing that everyone you serve by training will reach higher than you yourself do.

How Prophets Fit in the Five-Fold

We need the entire five-fold ministry operating in unity within the church, otherwise we risk building something for God that is unbalanced. Ephesians 2:20 talks about how the household of God (the church) is built upon the foundation of the apostles and prophets. You could say, Jesus the solid rock (Matthew 7:24-27) is presented by the evangelists. Upon the solid rock, the foundation is built by the apostles and prophets. Upon the foundation, the household of God is built and shaped by pastors and teachers. We can see that if we want to build for God's kingdom with lasting significance, then we need to see the fullness of God's leadership not only in action, but functioning in unity.

With every five-fold office there are strengths as well as blind spots. This is why God has called the five-fold ministry to work together as a team, instead of independently. In this chapter, I would like to shed light concerning how some of these different offices can work together with the prophetic office, how they complement one another, and what tensions may exist between them.

Prophets and Apostles

Ephesians 2:19-20: "Now, therefore, you are no longer strangers and foreigners, but fellow citizens with the saints and members of the household of God, having been built on the foundation of the apostles and prophets, Jesus Christ Himself being the chief cornerstone."

The apostolic and prophetic offices are a match made in heaven. When Paul the apostle would make a statement such as this saying that the household of God is built upon the foundation of the apostles and prophets, he didn't draw such conclusions simply through his experience. Paul was a theologian, and he understood that much of what was recorded in the Old Testament was a foreshadow of what Jesus would do in New Testament times. We can actually see strong parallels in how apostles and prophets would build together through how kings and prophets partnered with one another in the Old Testament.

The kings of Israel in many ways operated similar to how apostles function within the church today. This is true in the sense that kings in the Old Testament were the ones who provided the vision, governance, covering, and order to the culture of Israel, just as apostles do for the church. Just as kings and prophets co-laboured together to build foundations for Israel, so will apostles and prophets for the church.

In the Old Testament, prophets prophetically advised the king whom they served. This means they heard from God for those who He called to lead a nation. While the king received the initial vision for Israel, the prophet would then bring guidance by the word of the Lord in how that vision should be established. The same should be for apostles and prophets today. You could say that apostles receive the vision in God's heart concerning what to build for God's kingdom, and the prophet guides the apostle's hand as he or she builds.

I have seen many apostles try to build vision that God has given them without prophetic guidance. This usually leaves many blind spots in the structure of what is being established, because prophetic discernment is not keeping what is being built within the direct will of the Lord. Apostles often possess the gifts required to build for God's kingdom that prophets do not; yet prophets carry the ability to hear the Lord so the building can be done properly. God has created apostles and prophets to have a kingdom dependency upon one another.

Proverbs 29:18: "Where there is no vision, the people perish."

If you were to translate the word "vision" from Hebrew, this word literally means "prophetic vision." In spite of his fall in later years, king Solomon, the author of Proverbs was one of the most accomplished apostolic leaders in the Old Testament. What he wrote in this verse shows us that as an apostolic leader, he understood that ordinary vision was not enough to prevent people from perishing. They needed prophetic vision straight from the heart of God. King Solomon had a revelation of the importance in receiving from prophets to acquire prophetic direction and insight.

If a prophetic leader receives insight concerning vision and guidance for an apostolic leader, they need to understand what they are accountable for. As a prophetic person, if we receive this form of word for leadership, it is our job to take it to the Lord in prayer and to properly judge it, making sure it falls in line with proper prophetic etiquette. Once we do this and deliver the word, our job is done. Some prophetic people take on a false burden by trying to make their words come to pass. They try to control the leadership into the direction they feel things should go. This is manipulation, so we shouldn't have any part in this. The prophetic and apostolic relationship operates out of honour by respecting one another's capacity to lead in their entrusted office.

Remember the example of Paul and Agabus in Acts 21. Agabus warns Paul through a prophetic word, and Paul chose to go ahead with what he felt the Lord told him to do. Agabus didn't try to force Paul into doing what he thought he should do. He did his part as a prophet by judging the word, delivering it, and honouring Paul as an apostle.

We can see how an apostle's vision can falter without the help of a prophet, yet this partnership is two-sided. Apostles benefit prophets by showing them where and how they fit within in greater picture of God's plans. I have met far too many prophetic people who are lone-rangers, who try to single handedly advance God's kingdom. We were not created to build God's kingdom alone, but together with one another. Apostles carry the ability to make room for every type of ministry in the church, including the ministry of the prophetic and the office of a prophet.

We can see a very clear partnership of an apostle and prophet co-labouring together in New Testament times. We often overlook this, but Jesus and John the Baptist co-laboured together as an apostle and prophet throughout Israel. Jesus came as an apostle to present His vision given by the Father, which was that the kingdom of heaven would be established on the earth. John the Baptist's job as a prophet was to make straight the way of the Lord, so Jesus' apostolic vision could be established.

As an apostle and prophet, we can even see how Jesus and John the Baptist co-laboured that they could lay a proper foundation for us (Ephesians 2:20). 1 Corinthians 3:11 says, "For no other foundation can anyone lay than that which is laid, which is Jesus Christ."

Jesus the great Apostle laid himself down as the foundation for us to build the kingdom of heaven upon. John the Baptist did foundational work with Jesus as a prophet by making sure that every valley would be filled, and every mountain and hill brought low (Luke 3:5). John as a prophet prepared the way for Jesus, so that as our Great Foundation, He could properly lay upon a level land throughout Israel. This solid foundation that was laid by Jesus and John the Baptist, as an apostle and prophet, is the foundation that everything we now build for the kingdom is established upon.

Prophets and Evangelists

I have generally found that prophets and evangelists minister together quite naturally. Not only do they naturally mesh, but they are greatly beneficial to one another. Evangelists are very much driven by their passion and compassion towards others, especially those who do not know Jesus. Since they are gifted to be driven in such a way, one pitfall I have noticed that evangelists can easily slip into is submitting primarily to the will of their passion, instead of taking time to wait on the Lord for strategy. This will often lead evangelists to be driven by the needs of people, which could confuse their perception of the direction of God.

Prophets working alongside evangelists greatly counters this pitfall. When a prophet works alongside an evangelist, prophetic guidance can then narrow in an evangelist's passion to be directed where the Lord wants it. When this happens, all of a sudden the vision of an evangelist may look a lot less like a loose cannon firing in every direction, but becomes strategic and focused.

Another reason why there is wisdom for prophets and evangelists to work together, is because the prophetic ministry brings greater fruit in an evangelistic culture by empowering the ministry with the word of the Lord. For many of my highly evangelistic friends, the main giftings they function in while ministering to those who don't know Jesus is through prophecy and words of knowledge. A prophet can bring a very profound dynamic to an evangelistic ministry by training them to hear the word of the Lord more accurately. An evangelistic ministry apart from the gifts of the Spirit, is a ministry that will most likely try to lead people to truth through intellectual debates rather than through God's power. Since the world is hungry for a supernatural encounter with love, we need to learn to marry the prophetic ministry to how we reach the lost.

One of the ways the evangelistic office can benefit the prophetic office is by bringing application to what a prophet may be discerning or hearing the Lord say. You will often hear prophets prophesying about revival hitting different communities, cities, or nations. However, could you imagine the impact we would have as the church if a prophet could discern where God was going to move, and then communicate this to an evangelist so they could focus their outreach in that particular area? Evangelists and prophets working together could actually bring order, action, and application in bringing a prophet's word to come to pass.

Prophets and Pastors

While a prophetic office and a pastoral office can be greatly beneficial to one another, there can also be some tensions between the two. These tensions come into play when they are not functioning together under apostolic order and accountability.

A true pastor will have a heart to protect the people who are entrusted to them. So, when there are things taking place that are not common to a community, this can stir a protective posture in a pastoral leader. This protective posture takes shape out of a desire that people would not be hurt by what is unfamiliar. This is an amazing quality if what is not familiar are people who could cause congregation members harm, or the introduction of destructive doctrines. However, this posture is not good if we take it towards the things of Holy Spirit simply because they are outside our grid of comfort. Pastors are about protecting the people, whereas prophets are often about protecting the things of God. This is often where tension lies between pastors and prophets.

Since this is a common tension, it will often result in pastors holding prophets at a distance. While this distance could be created out of overprotectiveness from the pastor, it could also be the result of a prophet not understanding proper prophetic protocol. When a prophet or prophetic leader is misrepresenting the heart of God through the prophetic ministry, a pastor has every right to have their guard up.

These two ministries function together best under the anointing of the apostolic. Apostolic oversight and direction helps both the prophetic and pastoral find their intended places within the church. This is important, because if these two ministries cannot work together then it robs the church from experiencing the blessing of the prophetic ministry.

Even though there are tensions between these two offices, when they can co-labour together brilliant things can be accomplished. Pastors working with prophets helps to demystify the prophetic ministry because it brings a deeper level of revelation concerning relationships to the ministry. Pastors are also a great resource in accountability to prophets. Since isolation is a prominent pitfall for prophets, pastors can play a strong role in teaching prophets where they fit within community and in the family of God.

The pastoral ministry can benefit from the prophetic ministry because the gifts of the Spirit can greatly compliment things such as pastoral counselling and inner healing ministry. Pastors being trained by prophets to hear the voice of God can quicken their ability to minister to those who are entrusted to them. A word of knowledge or discernment can find root issues to unlock problems in the realm of the soul and in relationships.

Prophets and Teachers

In my opinion, prophets and teachers working together is a necessity. It is prophets who establish the value of the spoken word of God, and teachers enforce the value of the written word of God. Both are needed. Period.

There is an obvious tension between prophets and teachers. Prophets are more geared towards things that are potently spiritual and supernatural, whereas teachers are geared more towards analysis and intellectualism. While there is distinct contrast here, I believe God has created both offices with extreme strengths that cover one another's weaknesses.

Teachers assist prophets by keeping them grounded. I have met prophets who carry profound teaching gifts, and it is often crucial that they can bounce their new revelation and teachings off of Spirit-led teachers. I have seen prophets who try to teach apart from this form of accountability go down dark paths of false doctrines. This is one of the many reasons why prophets need to be relationally connected with teachers.

Teachers will also play a big role in helping prophets communicate the word of the Lord. Often, a prophet's priority is to receive the word of the Lord, and then to communicate it. Since this is a prophet's job, based on how they communicate, some may catch the word of the Lord while others may not. A teacher's job is more than just communicating a message; it is to make sure people understand the message. Teachers play a role in helping to demystify the prophetic word of the Lord so that it becomes palatable for everyone.

Another reason why prophets and teachers need to receive from one another is because prophets help train teachers not to become too intellectually dependent. When teachers are only intellectually dependent, they can have a tendency to dismiss anything that God may do that does not fit into their intellectual grid. This is dangerous, because then we risk reasoning ourselves out of experiencing what God may be doing. Prophets help equip teachers in how to allow the written word of God inside of them to become alive and active. Prophets guide teachers in how to marry their intellectual gifts with the gifts of the Spirit.

PROPHETIC PRAYER

If you have a heart to grow in your relationship with Jesus the Prophet, pray this prayer with me:

"Jesus, I receive You as my Prophet. I pray that You give me eyes to see what You are doing and ears to hear what You are saying. I pray that You expand my ability to hear You. Help me to hear You through Your still small quiet voice. Teach me to hear You through visions and dreams. I ask for Your voice to be clear to affirm, champion, and direct me. Raise me up to be a prophetic mouthpiece wherever You have called me."

OFFICE OF AN EVANGELIST

God is changing the ways that we expect revival will come. In the past we would pray for a move of the Spirit in a way as though expecting fire to fall from the sky. We would say that revival was just around the corner, but then sit back and wait for it to come. Here is where the shift is happening: while before we would sit back and wait for it to fall, we are now learning to steward revival in our heart. Therefore, instead of praying and waiting, we are now praying and releasing.

DEFINING AN EVANGELIST

We live in an incredible time. Like never before, there is a deep hunger crying out from the core of every man and woman to experience unconditional love. Since much of the world misinterprets what love actually is, many people seek out supernatural encounters through New Age and occultism. Practices such as palm reading, tarot card reading, and reiki healing are now all very common because of a lack of revelation concerning what a true supernatural encounter with love looks like. I'm sure many of us would like to blame society for the occult intruding our different cultures. Don't get me wrong, society certainly has a prominent part to play in this; however, I believe that we as the church have some part to play in the increased pursuit for counterfeit encounters. I believe this because as the church, we have in many ways laid aside our supernatural identities to primarily operate in an intellectual capacity. The power of the cross has been hidden by the church's obsessive pursuit of rational thought. We should be satisfying the world's hunger for the supernatural by demonstrating the power and love of Jesus. As this happens, people will quickly cast aside their interest in the counterfeit because we offer them the real thing. This is where evangelists come in.

The word "evangelist" has been used very loosely in the church. We often label anyone who has a deep love for those who don't know Jesus an evangelist, or say they have the gift of evangelism. Sorry to burst bubbles of comfort, but there is no gift of evangelism. Nor is everyone who loves the lost called as an evangelist. We are all called to love and reach the lost in the spheres of influence God has given us.

During my travels in ministry, I've met and worked with several evangelists. In fact, I find them very refreshing. The reason being, is that one thing burns within an evangelist's heart above all else: a passion for souls.

Several years ago when I was still new in ministry, I was serving a church helping them to get established as a body. As a leadership team, we recognized we were in a state of growth and realized our church needed training in several different areas. We needed to learn how to manage our time, how to build teams, and how to receive new vision. What we didn't realize at the time was that we needed someone apostolic to train us. Instead, we contacted a minister we heard of through the grapevine, inviting him to speak. What we didn't realize was that this man wasn't an apostle who could teach us how to build. This man was a full-blown evangelist.

As this minister spoke to us, it didn't matter what topic he started off with; by the end of his message he would be talking about evangelism. He would begin teaching a message about team building, yet somehow it would result in being about how to preach the gospel. He would talk about how to do healthy communication, yet his message would end by him sharing about how he led his flight attendant to the Lord on his way to our city. While our team was surprised to receive what we clearly didn't expect, this man walked in a radical love and undeniable power. He trained our people to manifest the heart of Jesus everywhere we went. The healings and salvations we saw through his impartation were amazing. It's no doubt the importance of us learning receiving from ministries such as this.

The term "evangelist" was only placed on one or two men in the early church, as recorded in scripture. The first mention of an evangelist was Philip in Acts 21:8, "On the next day we who were Paul's companions departed and came to Caesarea, and entered the house of Philip the evangelist, who was one of the seven, and stayed with him." The second use of the term was concerning Timothy when Paul wrote him in 2 Timothy 4:5 saying, "Do the work of an evangelist, fulfill your ministry." The fact that Timothy was not called an evangelist and was instead told to do the work of an evangelist makes me question if he actually had the office calling. Since Timothy was discipled by Paul, I can assume that he too was apostolic and was being directed by Paul to step into the ministerial role of an evangelist for a time.

Many evangelists are used as a direct spearhead to the mass population of those who do not yet know Jesus. When evangelists function in this capacity, they have an unusual favour with man from God and significant influence to impact the masses with the truth of the gospel. These men and women are the Billy Graham, Oral Roberts, and Jack Coe types. They are the ones who go where the gospel is scarce and have favour with man resting upon them to draw people to see mass salvations. This is where we can see we have gone wrong in terms of labelling everyone who does evangelism an evangelist. Our platform may be in the lives of people in our schools or work places, while an evangelist would more likely have platform from God with the masses.

There was a great acceleration of God raising up these types of evangelists during the Great Awakening, which took place in the 1700 and 1800's. One of the men who God had risen up in this time was John Wesley. He would stand under a tree and begin to share about Jesus as the masses would come to watch a man teaching about the cross and resurrection. Wonderful healings, deliverances, and other manifestations of the Spirit would take place as he spoke. John had a strong revelation of impartation, so he fathered hundreds of people to preach the gospel. Other men who flowed in this anointing who are worth the time to study were George Whitefield, Jonathan Edwards, Charles Finney, and D.L. Moody. These were all great men who diligently served the masses by laying down their lives for the gospel.

I've had the great privilege of working with many five-fold evangelists. Based on my experience with them and what I can see biblically, I believe we can see three primary characteristics that mark someone who truly walks in the office of an evangelist:

Evangelists Train in Evangelism

As stated in Ephesians 4:11-12, an evangelist's job isn't only to do evangelism. It is to train others to do evangelism. I'm not saying that an evangelist will teach people how to yell from street corners. Instead, they deposit within the church both passion and compassion towards those who don't yet know Jesus. They equip the church with power so we can be fruitful as we share about the love of God. There are certain gifts like healing and word of knowledge that gravitate to evangelists because they are excellent tools to bring people into a direct love encounter with Jesus. Through training and impartation, evangelists are called to impart love and gifting into the body of Christ so that the name of Jesus can be established throughout the nations.

1 Corinthians 2:4: "My (Paul's) message and my preaching were not with wise and persuasive words, but with a demonstration of the Spirit's power."

1 Corinthians 4:20: "For the kingdom of God is not in word but in power."

I have a very good friend who is a five-fold evangelist. He has laid his life down not only to see people saved, but also to train and equip the church to move in love and power. The amount of healings and salvations he has witnessed all throughout the world seem nearly endless. Over the years, he's had a strong emphasis on teaching the church to move in healing, deliverance, and words of knowledge. Currently, he leads evangelism teams to what is known as the darkest and most dangerous community in all of our nation.

I remember the first time this man stayed at our home. I can tell if someone is a true evangelist by how tangible their love for souls is. Since evangelists carry a grace to activate other people's evangelistic identity, just with him staying in our house, my wife and I could both feel our compassion for those who don't know Jesus increasing. Since I walk in more of a prophetic office, I've had many people comment that when they stay at our home their dream lives increase. So while my friend would stay at our home, I would come under his gift to be activated in evangelism, and he would experience an increase in his dreams and prophetic gifting. Our five-fold graces would literally rub off on one another! I find this rather amusing; but it shows how tangible the training and equipping gifts can actually be.

If you have a heart to reach those around you who don't know Jesus, I would encourage you to ask the Lord if there are any evangelists who you can learn from. God desires for each of us to be ready and mobile. He wants all of us to be moved by love and equipped with power.

Evangelists Set the Bar for Boldness

Acts 4:31: "When they had prayed, the place where they were assembled together was shaken; and they were all filled with the Holy Spirit, and they spoke the word of God with boldness."

The evangelists I know are by far some of the boldest people I've ever met. It is in many ways the inheritance of an evangelist. Just as a prophet's grace is to be able to hear the voice of God, an evangelist is called to impart their natural grace to the body of Christ, which is boldness.

Some might assume personality type has something to do with evangelists. Surely evangelists must be some of the most outgoing and extroverted people around. While this seems logical, Holy Spirit isn't dependent on personality types to use us. While I know many extroverted five-fold evangelists, I also know introverted ones as well.

Several years ago, I use to run an outreach ministry with a good friend of mine who is an evangelist. Not only is he an evangelist, but he is a highly introverted one. As for myself, I'm quite sure I'm the most introverted person I've encountered. My idea of a relaxing and energizing time is being tucked away in my office spending time with the Lord and writing books. In this particular outreach ministry we ran, I would train people to hear the voice of God, while he would equip them in evangelism. Here we were, two highly introverted individuals training the church to reach those who don't know Jesus. If that's not supernatural, then I don't know what is!

With this friend of mine in particular, I have always been challenged by his boldness. His personality has never been a stumbling block to him sharing about Jesus. In fact, I believe he's seen more healings outside the church during street evangelism than anyone I've ever met. Not only that, but the man's fire and boldness are highly infectious. Nearly everyone who comes around him is lit aflame, passion and compassion jousting them out from timidity.

I'm a firm believer that comfort zones are highly overrated. Growth takes risk. Faith takes risk; and risk is rarely comfortable. God wants to equip each of us with boldness, so our zeal will outweigh our desire for the familiar. Evangelists play a significant role in giving us a necessary push into the wild things of God.

Evangelists Determine the Church's Focus

Evangelists bring great balance to the other five-fold gifts. They do so by keeping us focused on the right thing. I believe that no matter what our ministry is, woven into our desired outcome needs to be that people who don't know Jesus will encounter Him. Evangelists help to establish this purpose.

Presently, I don't have a focus on leading outreaches. I leave this to evangelists since they are particularly gifted to do such things. My ministry is more geared towards training the church. That being said, I can't allow myself to become internally focused in my ministry. For everyone who I train in the prophetic ministry, I need to believe they will take what they've learned to impact those who don't know Jesus. Woven into the outcome of my ministry, I want to see fruit of people being saved. Thankfully, I've heard many testimonies of people reaching the lost through what I teach. If this weren't the case, I would be asking the Lord for new strategy. I believe the same could be said for any ministry. An apostle isn't called to build only to see the church encouraged. They need to build with the intent of seeing those who don't know Jesus impacted. A teacher teaches to equip the church to stand primarily as a light not in the church, but in a dark world. Pastors play a role in seeing people brought into wholeness; but it needs to be for the purpose of those people knowing how to be unshakable in a broken world. We can't allow ourselves to become too inward focused that we forget our mission.

I truly believe that if evangelists didn't exist, the church would struggle with being far too inwardly focused. The fire of an evangelist helps shift our eyes to see the great need in the world. Their boldness mobilizes us to rise from our pews, to get our hands working in the mission field. Their ability to train, equips us with the necessary tools so we can have as big of an impact as possible outside the four walls of the church.

COMMON PITFALLS
OF THE
EVANGELISTIC

The evangelistic ministry is an irreplaceable part of God's kingdom. However, if we are going to see it utilized to its full expression, we need to be aware of its potential pitfalls. Just like every ministry, it is beneficial when it is healthy, however it can also cause hurt and pain if it's not wielded with love and integrity. Over the years, I've had many friends who are evangelists, and those who are highly evangelistic. They've helped shed light for me to understand what pitfalls can follow the evangelistic ministry. Some of these pitfalls are struggles they've observed with others, as well as some they've personally learned to overcome.

Here are some pitfalls that can be experienced by evangelists and those who are highly evangelistic:

A Lack of Awareness of the Soul

As we go throughout life, I believe there is a balance we need to find concerning where our attention and focus lie. One of our eyes should be focused internally to examine our heart, keeping it in check. This is necessary for our emotional health and our relationship with the Lord. Our other eye should be outwards on the mission and mandate that lies before us. Just as highly pastoral people can struggle with having both eyes inward, overanalyzing the soul, evangelists can struggle with having both eyes outward on the mission. Having both eyes inward-focused is not heathy because then we are failing to see the mission. However, having both eyes outwards is not healthy either. Having both eyes outwards can often cause us to be blind to un-health that may be occurring within our soul. When this occurs, we may end up having external fruit, but the fruit of the Spirit is not taking shape within the core of our heart.

2 Corinthians 13:5: "Examine yourselves as to whether you are in the faith. Test yourselves."

Through his verse, God is giving us a responsibility to practice self-awareness. We are not supposed to have a blind eye to what is occurring within the hidden person of the heart. Holy Spirit wants to guide us to examine our heart, emotions, mindsets, motives, and actions. We are called to take up the responsibility to test ourselves to see if we are in full alignment with God's character, His word, and will.

When evangelists or highly evangelistic people are not willing to slow down to examine their hearts, they can end up running faster than what is healthy. This happens because drive and ambition are often something that evangelists naturally thrive in. If drive and ambition are not wielded by a healthy heart, it can cause an evangelist to run ahead of what God may want for them. It could cause them to step through doors or onto platform that their character cannot yet steward.

In everything we do, it is important to always remember to keep the motives of our heart in check. We should not allow ourselves to turn a blind eye to what is occurring in the soul. Refusing to be introspective can result in the greatest of giftings and anointings to become corrupt. It can steer strong drive and ambition to build for selfish reasons. Having a pure heart before the Lord should always be a primary priority.

I know many evangelists who have greatly avoided this pitfall. They have excelled in having one eye outwards on the mission, and one inwards on the soul. This is because they have made friendship with the Lord priority in their lives, intentionally inviting Jesus into every area of their heart. They have also built relationships with people who provide healthy-relational accountability.

Striving

When we are not able to see what is occurring internally within us, there can often be a struggle in receiving the love of God in the depths of our heart. This can often cause us to try to find our identity by striving. For evangelists, the enemy wants to blind them from wounding of the heart, so that they are doing evangelism and ministering as means to try to feel as though they have value in the eyes of God. This can result in highly evangelistic people ministering to the lost not from a place of love, but instead because they themselves do not feel loved or valued. This can create a destructive cycle of feeling as though they need to perform for God, in order to be received by Him.

If we place our identity in our ministry or career, then our drive to build will be fueled by a deep insecurity to find self-worth. It is in this place where we begin to submit to the will of our ego, instead of the will of the Lord. This can unfortunately lead to a place of burnout because we are not ministering from a place of rest, but instead out of an unhealthy perspective of ourselves and God.

Every one of us is in the process of working out of mentalities of orphan-ship, to understand we are a child of God. We live in the tension of moving from striving, to resting in His love. However, this process moves much quicker if we learn to slow down to allow the Lord to confront unhealthy motives in our heart. As we learn to be still before the Lord, He can correct and realign our heart much quicker. His heart is not for us to strive for His approval. We already have His approval because of the cross.

Ambition is an amazing gift from the Lord. However, it is properly anchored by ministering from a place of security in our identity, which can only be found in the love of God. It can only be found when we allow Him into the deep places of our heart.

Competition

1 Corinthians 12:26: "If one member suffers, all the members suffer with it; or if one member is honoured, all the members rejoice with it."

In the kingdom of God, we are called to champion one another to step into the fullness of what the Lord has called us to. Unfortunately, when we are unwilling to give our insecurities over to God, we can slip into a state of competition and jealously towards others. Competition and jealousy with evangelists can often be the result of slipping into the first pitfall of not being aware of what is occurring within our soul.

I want to specify something as I teach on this. It is fine to allow someone else's successes to spur us forwards. For the sake of example, what I mean by this is if a friend of yours has a strong anointing to see the sick healed, you can allow their breakthrough to push you to contend for the same thing. There is nothing wrong with this if we are at the same celebrating what the Lord is doing through them. Revelation 19:10 says, "The testimony of Jesus is the spirit of prophecy." This means that the testimony of what Jesus has done in someone else's life can be a prophetic word for us to receive. We begin to step into dangerous territory when we find ourselves preferring that we ourselves would have that breakthrough instead of others. We step into dangerous territory when we find ourselves wanting to one-up others with what the Lord has done in our lives. We need to reach a place where we can persevere into the things of God, as well as rejoice in other people's successes and promotions.

When our heart is plagued with competition and jealousy towards others, our drive can be fueled more by insecurity and one-upmanship rather than by love. Until we give these unhealthy mindsets over to God, He will often hold us back from stepping into new promotion, knowing that new platform and success will hurt us more than benefit us. God will often sacrifice the work to protect the worker. I have met many who are restless with their level of influence, yet God will not promote them because they haven't allowed Him to work competition and jealousy out of them. What is in our own heart can often be our greatest stumbling block from stepping into our full capacity. God wants to rid our heart from any competition or jealously that may be prevalent in us.

Isolation

Isolation can be a common pitfall for highly evangelistic people. Highly evangelistic people have a heart for the lost, which can often cause frustration towards lukewarmness in the church. This is not a bad quality. I have found myself frustrated with lukewarmness many times. However, what is not okay, is when we come to a place where we see other ministries and outlets of God's love as a form of lukewarmness simply because it doesn't always coincide with the urgency that highly evangelistic people feel to see people saved. This is something I have seen with many ministries, not only evangelistic ones. People who are highly gifted in one area can see more worth in the burden that the Lord has specifically given them, compared to other callings. Therefore, if people are not completely on board with their God-given burden or vision, they can perceive other ministries as less spiritual or effective. This is a mentality we need to throw out.

I will give you an example: say there is a pastor in a church who wants to build community within his church, so he decides to host a potluck. During the potluck, people are mingling, eating, and fellowshipping. Now, say there is a highly evangelistic person in that group. If this evangelistic person has not learned the value of a pastor's function, they may be thinking something along the lines of, "Why are we all just sitting around here joking, eating, and fellowshipping, when there are people out there suffering because they don't know Jesus?!"

Meanwhile, the pastor has an eye on the evangelistic person, thinking, "Why in the world is that person just sitting by themselves looking frustrated? Don't they see that we are trying to have fun? They're putting a damper on the whole event!"

A scenario like this is interesting because both ministries and desires are necessary. The evangelistic person needs to understand that there is great value in building community, whereas the pastor needs to understand that the evangelistic ministry brings passion to make the church mobile. We need to be able to see worth and necessity in each ministry that God has ordained. I have unfortunately met many people with great evangelistic callings who have abandoned the church entirely. In doing so, they have stepped into a lone-ranger mentality because they were at wits end with the church not doing what they feel they should be doing. Therefore, they leave and try to do their own thing.

Evangelists cannot singlehandedly see the world transformed. If we try to change the world by ourselves, we will only create sparks that will eventually fade. However, if we try to change the world together, we will play a part in birthing movements which will mark eternity. When evangelists isolate, they are actually limiting their capacity in advancing God's kingdom. God's heart is that the evangelistic ministry will find its place within the body of Christ.

Valuing Gifting more than Character

Something many of us have a tendency to do is place an overemphasis on what we ourselves are passionate about or gifted in. We do this because these things are a primary focus in our lives, so therefore assume it should be the same for everyone else. Since evangelists will often train and equip the church to move in power, there can be a great emphasis on miracles, signs, wonders, gifting, and anointing. There is nothing wrong with valuing such things. I believe we should have a strong emphasis on the supernatural things of the Spirit. I've spent years training and equipping the church to move in these very things. However, as important as they are, we should not see value in them alone.

We are treading dangerous waters when we only see value in the gifts of the Spirit (1 Corinthians 12:1-11), while overlooking the fruits of the Spirit (Galatians 5:22-23). This level of a lack of balance can be very destructive because it values one aspect of Holy Spirit, while rejects another. It celebrates gifting more than character. This mentality is especially destructive when it is woven into leadership. This trap naturally breeds a culture of competition, striving, performance, and overlooking dysfunction. We should be greatly driven to move in the gifts of the Spirit. Scripture demands it (1 Corinthians 14:1). However, we should be equally as driven, if not more so to walk in the fruits of the Spirit.

The most impactful and influential evangelists I have worked with understand this greatly. They understand that we cannot give love that we haven't personally received. This is why they spend much time allowing God to shape the fruit of the Spirit in their heart, knowing this is what will help them to live out their calling with longevity. Not only is it beneficial for them personally, but also for those who they are called to train and equip. The wholeness and balance they exemplify in their own lives is what is imparted to those they mentor and disciple. When evangelists have a high value for the fruits of the Spirit, it will always result in multiplication in their external fruit to see those who do not yet know Jesus impacted be the love of God.

HOW
EVANGELISTS FIT
IN THE FIVE-FOLD

We need the entire five-fold ministry operating in unity within the church, otherwise we risk building something for God that is unbalanced. Ephesians 2:20 talks about how the household of God (the church) is built upon the foundation of the apostles and prophets. You could say, Jesus the solid rock (Matthew 7:24-27) is presented by the evangelists. Upon the solid rock, the foundation is built by the apostles and prophets. Upon the foundation, the household of God is built and shaped by pastors and teachers. We can see that if we want to build for God's kingdom with lasting significance, then we need to see the fullness of God's leadership not only in action, but functioning in unity.

With every five-fold office there are strengths as well as blind spots. This is why God has called the five-fold ministry to work together as a team, instead of

endently. In this chapter, I would like to shed
ht concerning how some of these different offices
can work together with the evangelistic office, how
they complement one another, and what tensions may
exist between them.

Evangelists and Apostles

It is crucial that apostles and evangelists work
together, even though there can often be tension in this
ministerial relationship. This tension often lies within
apostles not understanding the function of an
evangelist and evangelists fearing being controlled.

Evangelists carry a reputation for being the wild-
child of the five-fold ministry; however, this is not a
poor quality. Evangelists are the ones who are called to
help make the church mobile. A part of their gift to the
church is to be wild and out of the box. When apostles
do not understand an evangelist's role within the five-
fold ministry, they could slip into a mentality of trying
to control an evangelist's expression. This often results
in evangelists trying to minister independently from the
local church, taking an independent stance in ministry
instead of a unified one. Health is brought to this
relationship when the apostolic functions from this
principle: a true apostolic ministry does not control, it
sends out.

We can see a brilliant example of apostles and
evangelists working together in Acts 8. Phillip the
evangelist was sent out to go before the apostles to a
territory where knowledge of the Lord was scarce. He

would minister in miracles, signs, and wonders, thus seeing mass salvations. We can then see that the apostles would follow up with the ministry that Phillip would do. The apostles would go to bring stability to what Phillip birthed, so that it could last with longevity. Phillip would spark the first flame, and the apostles would make sure the flame did not die out by bringing order to the movement. Apostles made sure that the evangelist's spark would become a wildfire for kingdom advancement.

As apostles understand the role of evangelists and learn to healthily release them, we begin to see the kingdom of God stretching beyond the four walls of the church. Evangelists actually benefit apostles by expanding apostolic vision to wherever they preach the gospel. Evangelists also help apostles in remembering that their grand vision needs to always point towards reaching those who do not yet know Jesus.

Evangelists can often struggle with understanding their placement within the local church. This is where apostles can greatly benefit evangelists. Since apostles carry a grace to understand the big picture of God's kingdom, they can lead evangelists to understand where they fit within the body of Christ. It is in this place of partnership, accountability, and relationship where we can see these two ministries function at a more complete capacity.

Evangelists and Prophets

I have generally found that prophets and evangelists minister together quite naturally. Not only do they naturally mesh, but they are greatly beneficial to one another. Evangelists are very much driven by their passion and compassion towards others, especially those who do not know Jesus. Since they are gifted to be driven in such a way, one pitfall I have noticed that evangelists can easily slip into is submitting primarily to the will of their passion, instead of taking time to wait on the Lord for strategy. This will often lead evangelists to be driven by the needs of people, which could confuse their perception of the direction of God.

Prophets working alongside evangelists greatly counters this pitfall. When a prophet works alongside an evangelist, prophetic guidance can then narrow in an evangelist's passion to be directed where the Lord wants it. When this happens, all of a sudden the vision of an evangelist may look a lot less like a loose cannon firing in every direction, but becomes strategic and focused.

Another reason why there is wisdom for prophets and evangelists to work together, is because the prophetic ministry brings greater fruit in an evangelistic culture by empowering the ministry with the word of the Lord. For many of my highly evangelistic friends, the main giftings they function in while ministering to those who don't know Jesus is through prophecy and words of knowledge. A prophet can bring a very profound dynamic to an evangelistic ministry by training them to hear the word of the Lord more accurately. An evangelistic ministry apart from the gifts of the Spirit, is a ministry that will most likely try to lead people to truth through intellectual debates rather than through God's power. Since the world is hungry for a supernatural encounter with love, we need to learn to marry the prophetic ministry to how we reach the lost.

One of the ways the evangelistic office can benefit the prophetic office is by bringing application to what a prophet may be discerning or hearing the Lord say. You will often hear prophets prophesying about revival hitting different communities, cities, or nations. However, could you imagine the impact we would have as the church if a prophet could discern where God was going to move, and then communicate this to an evangelist so they could focus their outreach in that particular area? Evangelists and prophets working together could actually bring order, action, and application in bringing a prophet's word to come to pass.

Evangelists and Pastors

Even though there are some tension points between evangelists and pastors, they benefit one another greatly. The tension often lies with evangelists often wishing pastors were more focused on the lost, whereas pastors often desire that evangelists had a greater grasp on community. However, it is these very differences that sharpen the other.

Pastors can slip into a mentality of having both eyes inwards to examine the heart. While examining the heart is a good thing, we need to also have one eye out on the mission before us. This is how evangelists help pastors. They shift one of their eyes outwards to what the Lord is doing externally. While pastors will always be more primarily gifted in pastoring, it is also important for them to have a heart for what the Lord is doing beyond the four walls of the church.

Pastors greatly benefit evangelists in many ways. The first is that pastors can help evangelists in staying in a place of health in their soul. Just as pastors can have a tendency of having both eyes inward, evangelists can struggle with having both eyes outward on the mission. This can often cause evangelists to be blind to a lack of health that may be occurring within their soul. Pastors can help evangelists to stay in a place of emotional health so they can live out their calling with longevity. Pastors also greatly benefit evangelists in understanding health in relationships. This is very important considering isolation is a very common pitfall for evangelists. Just as apostles will teach evangelists how they fit within the grand picture of the kingdom, pastors will teach evangelists how they fit within community.

We can clearly see that pastors and evangelists bring health to one another. When pastors and evangelists work together, pastors begin to play a key role to relationally disciple those who evangelists are bringing to the Lord.

Evangelists and Teachers

Even though the function of evangelists and teachers look completely different, they are greatly complimentary to one another. One of the tension points between evangelists and teachers lies with the fact that their individual roles are on the opposite ends of the spectrum. Evangelists thrive in the place of risk. They are moved by passion to see people encounter the supernatural love of God outside the church. Teachers are often quite intellectual in how they understand the things of God. Therefore, they will often be more utilized by God within the four walls of the church. Even though they are different, both roles are irreplaceable in the kingdom of God and are very beneficial to one another.

While evangelists are often focused on those who do not know Jesus, teachers take a role of equipping individuals once they transition into knowing Christ. As evangelists and teachers begin to work alongside one another, not only do we see people saved, but we see them discipled. As evangelists are playing a role in bringing people to the Lord, teachers can then begin to teach these people the foundation truths of God. This leads them into allowing the Lord by laying a foundation of who He is in their lives. Teachers working with those who are new to knowing God, quickens them to a place of maturity.

EVANGELISTIC PRAYER

If you have a heart to grow in your relationship with Jesus the Evangelist, pray this prayer with me:

"Jesus, I receive You as my Evangelist. I pray that You give me a heart for those who don't yet know You. Use me as a light to manifest Your love. I pray for a revelation of Your power. I ask for an impartation from heaven to move in healings, deliverance, and words of knowledge. Let me be a sign and wonder to those who I encounter. Let me be an administrator of Your love throughout the earth."

OFFICE OF A PASTOR

The move of God taking place throughout the earth, isn't only about miracles, signs, and wonders; it's also about whole hearts, healthy relationships, and thriving marriages.

DEFINING A PASTOR

While I consider the apostolic office the "forgotten office of the five-fold" I believe the pastoral office is the most misunderstood. Due to a lack of understanding of the five-fold ministry, in many ways, the full burden of Ephesians 4:11-12 has been placed upon the shoulders of the pastor. So much so, that pastors have been expected to operate as the full embodiment of the five-fold ministry. We have expected pastors to have the most vision for their church, like an apostle would; and expected them to be the best at hearing God's voice, like a prophet. We've expected them to have the biggest heart for their community, as an evangelist would; and expected them to teach every Sunday, as though they were a teacher. We've expected pastors to fulfill five roles, and then we wonder why so many of them burnout! However, we are transitioning into a time where the church is ready to receive the rest of God's leadership, meaning that pastors will be relieved from this unrealistic expectation.

While teachers walk as the representation of Jesus the Rabbi, pastors get the privilege to minister as representatives of Jesus the Shepherd. Teachers take more of a role in watering the church, whereas pastors lean more towards protecting and nurturing the people. One of the best descriptions of a pastor I have found in the New Testament is in the book of Acts.

Acts 6:1-3: "Now in those days, when the number of the disciples was multiplying, then arose a complaint against the Hebrews by the Hellenists, because their widows were neglected in the daily distribution. Then the twelve summoned the multitude of the disciples and said, 'It is not desirable that we should leave the word of God and serve tables. Therefore, brethren, seek out from among you seven men of good reputation, full of the Holy Spirit and wisdom, whom we may appoint over this business.'"

I believe that these seven appointed by the apostles were the first to walk in a pastoral function in the early church. Most peoples' understanding of a pastor's primary anointing is to prepare and share the message with the church, when to be honest I don't even think it's necessary for a pastor to have to be the one to share on a Sunday morning, unless God has called and anointed him or her to do so. While a teacher might spend the bulk of his ministry in studying and teaching, the pastor's burden is to be in amongst the people taking care of practical, relational, and emotional needs. They are the ones who determine the emotional and relational health of the church. They will be the ones who are making sure everyone in the congregation has enough money to buy groceries, making hospital visits to spend time with those who are sick, and are willing to walk husbands and wives through relational issues. They stand as protectors and peacemakers amongst the church, just as a shepherd protects the sheep from the wolves and establishes peace amongst the sheep so that they can live together as one unit. A true five-fold pastor will make sure they aren't the only ones functioning pastorally, but will focus on training others to carry a pastoral heart.

During my speaking endeavors over the years, I've had the privilege of working with pastors all around the world. I've spoken at many of their churches, trained their people, and built with them. Here are three primary functions of a five-fold pastor that I've observed.

Pastors Tend to the Soul

A part of the pastoral ministry is building Christ within the souls of individuals by bringing emotional balance and healing. This is why the pastors that were appointed in Acts 6 were called to take care of the widows. Pastors have a deep compassion and drive to connect the broken-hearted with the Father. The root revelation that pastors minister from is of the Father's love. Since this is the pastor's mandate, they will often be involved in walking people through their heart issues through counselling, inner healing sessions, or by living day-by-day with people in relationship. With pastors it is unmistakable that they are willing to get their hands dirty to see people healed and set free. While I've met many pastors who do this in a one-on-

one scale, I've also met others who pastorally train and equip the masses to be healthy in their soul through travelling, speaking, and writing.

While my wife doesn't refer to herself as a five-fold pastor, as far as bringing healing to the broken hearted she is undeniably one of the most pastoral people I've ever met. As a pastor does, she has an amazing gift to bring healing to the brokenhearted. I can't even count how many times we've been at a restaurant together and she will strike up a conversation with our waiter or waitress. After only a few minutes of my wife probing them with questions, they will be telling her things about their lives that they've never told anyone. She's someone who has encountered Jesus the Pastor in her own life to such a degree that people who she doesn't even know consider her to be a safe place with their deepest processes.

An ability to journey with people into wholeness is one of the staples of the pastoral ministry. Since a pastor's job is so hands-on relationally, I think it's a practical statement to say that there should be one person to every twenty people or so to closely pastor them. This of course will vary depending on the person. However, I say this because all of our relational bandwidths have a limit. Those who are not overly gifted pastorally, know that walking with even one person who is working through deep emotional wounding can be a challenging thing at times. I have a deep respect for large churches that have many pastors because I then know that the congregation's practical and emotional needs are taken into deep consideration. If pastors are taken out of the equation of the five-fold ministry, then neglect sneaks into churches and we can end up with a group of people who feel greatly overlooked.

Pastors Build Community

Pastors have authority in several realms. One is in the place of the soul; another is in relationships. Pastors have a supernatural ability to create community. Have you ever met someone who can walk in a room full of strangers and make them a community? If so, then you've likely met someone who is highly pastoral.

Jesus was the greatest Pastor who ever walked the earth. Let's take a look at the twelve disciples for instance: Jesus' disciple Andrew was Peter's brother. He was a fisherman and originally was a disciple of John the Baptist (Mark 1:16-18). James, John, and Peter were all fishermen. Many scholars believe that Nathaniel was the only disciple who came from royal blood, or noble birth. They believe this because his name means "son of Talmai". Talmai was king of Geshur whose daughter, Maacah, was the wife of David, mother of Absalom (2 Samuel 3:3). Simon was a zealot, which was a conspiracy group that revolted against the government. Many scholars believe Jude was also part of this group. Matthew was a tax collector. This was an extremely random group of men; most of whom were strangers to one another.

This is astounding to me. Jesus picked a man who was from royal blood and threw him with a bunch of fishermen, which was one of the lowliest trades in that time. He grabbed a tax collector who worked for the government and put him together with two zealots. Jesus brought together twelve people who didn't only have different personalities, but had completely different ideologies altogether. They all perceived life through entirely different lenses, yet Jesus brought them together to teach them how to be a family. Jesus as a Pastor taught them how to live life amongst one another because they were called to be Jesus' successors in leading the revival that redirected history. Sometimes we forget that the same twelve disciples who walked with Jesus in the gospels, were the same twelve apostles who led the church in Acts, minus Judas. Worldwide revival was actually dependent on whether or not Jesus could teach the twelve to put aside their differences and be a family.

I believe the last supper is one of the most beautiful depictions of unity and fellowship written in the Bible. We see twelve people eating together who from a realistic point of view should not be in relationship with one another. Throughout the gospels we can see how the disciples clearly didn't get along all of the time. In fact, there are several accounts of them arguing amongst each other. Considering their differences how could they not? Nathaniel being a nobleman, could have clashed with Peter, James, and John since they were fishermen and may have been on the rougher side in their personalities. Matthew, being a tax collector could have had problems with superiority, and the zealots more than likely had severe authority issues. Yet, they could live life together because they met around Jesus their Pastor. He was their common ground to relate and love one another.

Back in Biblical times, often people would not get together to eat with just anyone. Fellowshipping over food was something special. In that time and culture people would often only eat with those who they were committed to living life with. The communion is a picture of twelve men who committed to living life with one another. Jesus brought these men together and taught them to love one another in spite of their differences to the point where they could commit to each other and be a family. While at first, Jesus had to stand as the mediator between the disciples, by the time He ascended to heaven, they loved each other so much that they could operate as a healthy family to steward a move of God. This type of community, family, and health in relationships is the fruit of a true pastor.

Pastors Protect

A true pastor will protect those entrusted to them by any means necessary. Every local church is like its own little family. While the apostolic provides necessary oversight, a pastor is the one who keeps the house in order, making sure it's healthy and safe for every member.

Working with pastors, I've seen first-hand their tenacious desire to protect. It is a desire both admirable and understandable. Many pastors I know have walked with the same people for over a decade. They've journeyed with these people through their highs and lows; through issues of the heart, trials, and marital issues. Whether threats come in the form of wolves in sheep's clothing, sin within the church, or issues of the heart, a true pastor comes around the church like a shield to guard and protect.

No matter who we are in the body of Christ, it is important to be under the accountability of pastoral counsel in our relationships, work, or ministry. We need people around us who know how to guard and protect. Since there's is a specific grace for pastors to understand matters of the heart, they can provide a second set of internal eyes to help examine what is happening in the realm of the soul. Pastors don't only guard us from external threat; accountability to a true pastor can protect us from any threats that could potentially rise even from our own heart.

When we receive ministry from a true pastor, not only should we become healthier emotionally, but we will also become pastoral ourselves. Since a pastor is called to train and equip the body of Christ, when we walk in relationship with a pastor we ourselves can learn to walk in a pastoral anointing. This of course doesn't mean we ourselves are five-fold pastors; but that we will do the work of a pastor in the spheres of influence where God has entrusted us.

COMMON PITFALLS
OF THE PASTORAL

The pastoral ministry is an irreplaceable part of God's kingdom. However, if we are going to see it utilized to its full expression, we need to be aware of its potential pitfalls. Just like every ministry, it is beneficial when it is healthy, however it can also cause hurt and pain if it's not wielded with love and integrity. Over the years, I've worked with pastors all over the world. They've helped shed light for me to understand what pitfalls can follow the pastoral ministry. Some of these pitfalls are struggles they've observed with others, as well as some they've personally learned to overcome.

Here are some pitfalls that can be experienced by pastors and those who are highly pastoral people:

Lack of Boundaries

Since pastors carry such a strong grace for bringing healing to the broken hearted, they will often be a magnet to those who need deep inner healing. This is a normal occurrence considering that pastors carry authority in the realm of the soul. Something every pastoral person needs to know while working with those who need healing in the heart, is that we cannot try to work harder on someone than they are willing to work on themselves. This is a crucial principle to know, considering many leaders have experienced burnout by trying to take on this responsibility. The reason why many have suffered from burnout in this process, is because they end up running in circles, tiring themselves out by working harder than the person who actually needs the healing.

We need to remember that our relational and ministerial bandwidth has a limit, therefore we need to be discerning concerning who to walk with. Even though a pastor's relational bandwidth may be broader than others, just like everyone else, pastors need to have boundaries in their relationships. God wants pastors to be in this for the long hall, so therefore they need to be willing to put up healthy boundaries to protect their time and energy.

I once heard a man of God say, "One of the quickest ways that the enemy will try to burn someone out is by surrounding them with a large amount of people who are unwilling to work on their heart issues." I have held this statement of wisdom close to the heart. Even though I'm not primarily pastoral, I do have a deep love for people. Therefore, I need to make sure I'm guarding my time wisely. I do this by not only investing into those who honour my time, but by only sowing into those who I feel Holy Spirit directing me to do so with.

Unfortunately, I haven't only seen pastors burnout due to a lack of boundaries, but I've also seen their families suffer greatly because of it. I've seen pastors who have had very caring hearts for people, yet since all their time was put into ministry, their children didn't feel shepherded by their parents. This resulted in the children turning away from the Lord because of neglect. It is amazing how when our strengths are not under full submission to the will of God, the enemy will try to use them against us.

As a pastoral person it is very attainable to have healthy boundaries with ministry and people. I have many friends in pastoral ministry who minister very well without slipping into this pitfall. They are some of the healthiest individuals I know. Their families love God and they are seeing God's kingdom advancing powerfully.

Tolerance of Dysfunction

Pastors have profound compassion for those they shepherd. Not only do they have compassion, but also great empathy. Empathy is the ability to emotionally feel and understand what others are going through. This is a powerful gift from the Lord, as it requires a deep love for people. When empathy is not harnessed by wisdom from the Lord, it can lead to a dangerous place. Walking in empathy apart from wisdom can result in our emotion clouding our discernment. This can often cause us to see people's potential to such a degree that we overlook dysfunction. Please don't mistake what I'm saying, we are always called to see potential. However, there is also wisdom in realistically understanding where someone is currently at as well.

Embracing empathy apart from wisdom has unfortunately allowed a form of passivity in the church. This passivity in a lot of ways has allowed a foothold of un-health within the local church. It is this pitfall that causes leaders to promote people into places of leadership where they shouldn't be. It is this pitfall that tolerates harmful behaviour. I understand that we are all on a journey growing into wholeness; however, if someone is a sexual predator and is unwilling to be brought to repentance, they should not be put in a place of leadership out of a fear of them leaving the church. This is not loving or safe to those in the church. True love would protect people from this type of dysfunctional behaviour. It is unfortunately not uncommon for harmful and dangerous people to be promoted into places of leadership because their oversight is afraid that they would feel rejected. We absolutely need to make people feel as though they belong, but not at the expense of the safety of others who are entrusted to us to protect.

When the apostle John wrote the church of Thyatira in Revelation 2:20, he said, "Nevertheless I have a few things against you, because you allow that woman Jezebel, who calls herself a prophetess, to teach and seduce my servants to commit sexual immorality and eat things sacrificed to idols."

The church of Thyatira was held accountable for their passivity of tolerating the practices of Jezebel. A true pastor will defend his or her sheep by any means necessary, even if it means being blunt and straightforward at times. Shepherds cannot always be soft, otherwise they will not do their job correctly in protecting the sheep.

Literal shepherds hold a shepherding rod with a large crook on the end of it. If one of the shepherd's sheep begins to wander away from the pack, then the shepherd will put the rod around the sheep's neck to yank it back into line. This isn't a method of control; it protects the sheep from being eaten by wolves. There has been a false teaching that has crept into the church saying that every leader needs to always be extremely "nice" in order to be Christ-like. To be kind and to be nice are two different things. Niceness is not a fruit of the Spirit. Since this mindset has infected many leaders, those who look up to them have begun to walk in the same pattern which has brought passivity into the body. As long as we are passive, we will never be able to take care of what has been given to us. Adam made the same mistake when his bride, Eve, ate from the tree of knowledge of good and evil. Instead of embracing conflict and taking a stand to stop her, he became passive and just watched her eat the fruit.

As leaders we need to have a leadership style that reflects both the Lion and the Lamb. If we are only gentle like a lamb unable to confront the issues at hand, then people will undermine our authority in leadership and walk all over us. Not only will we be swept under the rug as leaders, but people will end up being pulled from truth by wolves and will end up getting hurt. That being said, if we are only bold and direct like a lion then people will leave feeling hurt and wounded not by the wolves, but by us the leaders. We need to be well rounded as leaders, being both compassionate enough to listen, and passionate enough to declare truth. We need to allow Jesus the Lion and the Lamb to be formed and fashioned within us.

Unhealthy Co-dependency

You may think that I'm about to write about not allowing church members to have unhealthy co-dependencies towards pastoral leaders, right? We do need to try to prevent those who we lead from having an unhealthy dependency on us; however, right now I'm going to share from the opposite spectrum.

If a pastoral leader is walking in deep insecurity, there can at times be an unhealthy level of co-dependency that can form in their hearts toward those who they are pastoring. This takes place when pastors find their identity in the fact that they are "needed" by others. A pastor needs to always remember that they are a son or daughter of God, before they are a pastor. This means they do not need to find their security and worth in those who they lead, but in the Father.

In more severe cases, when pastors have an unhealthy soul-tie to those who they lead, there can be an incessant need to feel wanted, so therefore they can take a controlling posture to feel secure. This can often come across as undermining others to appear more spiritually mature. Individuals being "pastored" in such a way will have great difficulties growing into a place of maturity, because they are essentially being looked down upon by a spiritual leader, and are being spiritually micromanaged.

We can see a good analogy of this in a parent and child relationship:

When a child is young, they need to be cared for and parented to a great degree. They need to be told how to do many basic things in life, because they have not lived it yet. However, once the child grows into an adult, they don't need to be parented in the same manner. Parenting becomes more hands-off, because as an adult, they don't need to be walked with as closely. If a parent continues to treat their son or daughter as though they are not capable of walking independently, they will respond in one of two ways. They will either create distance with the parent due to a fear of being controlled, or they will submit to the micromanaging, embracing a lie that they are indeed not capable of living life independently from their parent. The latter results in stunted growth for the son or daughter even though they are an adult.

This is what this type of pastoring can do. It may make the pastor feel good about themselves; however, it cripples those who they are pastoring in their ability to grow up spiritually. This type of leadership actually puts a stop in people's lives from making a large impact for the kingdom of heaven. A true pastor will instead be able to raise those they pastor to a place of spiritual maturity, so they can healthily be sent out to fulfill their God-given calling and mandate.

Worship of Community

There is a powerful wave of revelation hitting the church concerning understanding the family of God. The bar for kingdom relationships is being risen in the church, which is resulting in many in the body of Christ coming to a newfound revelation of belonging. Five-fold pastors have had a significant part to play in helping to deposit such a profound revelation. That being said, every time God releases fresh revelation to the church, the enemy's goal is to try to pull that revelation to an unhealthy extreme.

The unhealthy extreme we need to watch out for is a worship of community. Community is a powerful and necessary thing if we are to see God's kingdom established on the earth. In fact, I have trained and taught a great amount concerning kingdom relationships throughout the years. However, as the church, we need to remember that we are not called to meet around community; we are called to meet around the presence of Jesus.

When we primarily meet around community instead of presence, there are several skewed mentalities we can slip into. One of the most dangerous ones I've seen is we can stop viewing church as a place where God can supernaturally show up at any time. I truly believe God wants to restore reverence and wonder back to the local church. Is church a place where we come to find community? Absolutely. However, it is also a place where we can come to encounter the living God. I believe when we come to church, we should be enshrouded together in God's presence. In this place, anything can happen. The sick are healed. Self-hatred, depression, and fear are dethroned. The saints are trained. This is what happens when we gather around presence.

A pastoral culture of community and relationships is key to what God wants to do in the earth; but in our heart, community should never trump the presence of the Lord. Our focus should instead be to become a dwelling place for His presence. In this place we will begin to naturally see kingdom relationships unfold.

Fear Towards Holy Spirit

This pitfall builds very easily off of the one prior. The reason being is that a worshipful heart towards community will often result in a fear towards Holy Spirit. As soon as we begin to worship community, we will start to hold it at a higher place of importance than the presence of God, which is a very dangerous mindset to walk in. No matter who we are, our primary priority should be to know God. When we put community above encountering Him in His presence, we will immediately step into trying to control Holy Spirit to appease to other people's comfort. This is how we end up with churches or ministries that function more seeker friendly, instead of Spirit-friendly. We begin to have a very high value for people's comfort, at the expense of what Holy Spirit may want to do.

One of the expressions of the shepherding anointing is to protect the sheep from danger. It is to guard people from the schemes of the enemy, and to create a culture where people can grow in the Lord; it is not to protect them from Holy Spirit. In my experience with pastoring and doing itinerant ministry, if we are trying to lead people to a place of maturity, then it is wise to create an atmosphere in church where they could potentially have an experience with God, Himself. This means valuing the presence of God and the leading of Holy Spirit. This is far more fruitful than tiptoeing around the person of Holy Spirit, worrying about people being offended. People are transformed far quicker in the presence of Jesus than they are in manmade wineskins.

How Pastors Fit
in the Five-Fold

We need the entire five-fold ministry operating in unity within the church, otherwise we risk building something for God that is unbalanced. Ephesians 2:20 talks about how the household of God (the church) is built upon the foundation of the apostles and prophets. You could say, Jesus the solid rock (Matthew 7:24-27) is presented by the evangelists. Upon the solid rock, the foundation is built by the apostles and prophets. Upon the foundation, the household of God is built and shaped by pastors and teachers. We can see that if we want to build for God's kingdom with lasting significance, then we need to see the fullness of God's leadership not only in action, but functioning in unity.

With every five-fold office there are strengths as well as blind spots. This is why God has called the five-fold ministry to work together as a team, instead of independently. In this chapter, I would like to shed light concerning how some of these different offices can work together with the pastoral office, how they complement one another, and what tensions may exist between them.

Pastors and Apostles

There has been an unfortunate lack of apostles and pastors working together. This is often due to the fact that we have in many ways laid the apostolic office to the wayside, and have expected pastors to pick up the mandate of governance in churches and ministries. Biblically, we can see the Jesus rose up apostles to take a role of governance in the church. This is why he invested into and commissioned the twelve apostles, not the twelve pastors.

A pastor's realm of authority in training the church is in the soul and in relationships. Since this is the case, there is something very interesting that occurs when we have pastoral oversight instead of apostolic governance in churches or ministries. Since pastors are in many ways internally focused, we have very internally focused churches. We end up with ministries that have very healthy people emotionally, socially, and relationally; however, we easily forget about the grander mission of the kingdom of heaven invading earth. Extreme pastoral cultures that do not have an apostolic revelation will often step into a posture that isolates the church from having a grand kingdom impact in society.

Apostles have a revelation of the grander mission of the kingdom of heaven. Apostles bring great balance to pastors because they don't only think about internal health, but also outward impact. An apostle's mandate is to train the church how to advance God's kingdom in every person's sphere of influence. This is why pastors function more healthily under apostolic accountability, compared to apostles submitting to pastoral headship. In God's biblical order, an apostolic leader would be providing governance so that the vision of a church or ministry can remain on track with the will of God. In this place, pastors can shepherd individuals into freedom, wholeness, and in how to walk in relationships so we can have healthy people advancing God's kingdom everywhere they go.

Pastors and Prophets

While a prophetic office and a pastoral office can be greatly beneficial to one another, there can also be some tensions between the two. These tensions come into play when they are not functioning together under apostolic order and accountability.

A true pastor will have a heart to protect the people who are entrusted to them. So, when there are things taking place that are not common to a community, this can stir a protective posture in a pastoral leader. This protective posture takes shape out of a desire that people would not be hurt by what is unfamiliar. This is an amazing quality if what is not familiar are people who could cause congregation members harm, or the introduction of destructive doctrines. However, this posture is not good if we take it towards the things of Holy Spirit simply because they are outside our grid of comfort. Pastors are about protecting the people, whereas prophets are often about protecting the things of God. This is often where tension lies between pastors and prophets.

Since this is a common tension, it will often result in pastors holding prophets at a distance. While this distance could be created out of overprotectiveness from the pastor, it could also be the result of a prophet not understanding proper prophetic protocol. When a prophet or prophetic leader is misrepresenting the heart of God through the prophetic ministry, a pastor has every right to have their guard up.

These two ministries function together best under the anointing of the apostolic. Apostolic oversight and direction helps both the prophetic and pastoral find their intended places within the church. This is important, because if these two ministries cannot work together then it robs the church from experiencing the blessing of the prophetic ministry.

Even though there are tensions between these two offices, when they can co-labour together brilliant things can be accomplished. Pastors working with prophets helps to demystify the prophetic ministry because it brings a deeper level of revelation concerning relationships to the ministry. Pastors are also a great resource in accountability to prophets. Since isolation is a prominent pitfall for prophets, pastors can play a strong role in teaching prophets where they fit within community and in the family of God.

The pastoral ministry can benefit from the prophetic ministry because the gifts of the Spirit can greatly compliment things such as pastoral counselling and inner healing ministry. Pastors being trained by prophets to hear the voice of God can quicken their ability to minister to those who are entrusted to them. A word of knowledge or discernment can find root issues to unlock problems in the realm of the soul and in relationships.

Pastors and Evangelists

Even though there are some tension points between evangelists and pastors, they benefit one another greatly. The tension often lies with evangelists often wishing pastors were more focused on the lost, whereas pastors often desire that evangelists had a greater grasp on community. However, it is these very differences that sharpen the other.

Pastors can slip into a mentality of having both eyes inwards to examine the heart. While examining the heart is a good thing, we need to also have one eye out on the mission before us. This is how evangelists help pastors. They shift one of their eyes outwards to what the Lord is doing externally. While pastors will always be more primarily gifted in pastoring, it is also important for them to have a heart for what the Lord is doing beyond the four walls of the church.

Pastors greatly benefit evangelists in many ways. The first is that pastors can help evangelists in staying in a place of health in their soul. Just as pastors can have a tendency of having both eyes inward, evangelists can struggle with having both eyes outward on the mission. This can often cause evangelists to be blind to a lack of health that may be occurring within their soul. Pastors can help evangelists to stay in a place of emotional health so they can live out their calling with longevity. Pastors also greatly benefit evangelists in understanding health in relationships. This is very important considering isolation is a very common pitfall for evangelists. Just as apostles will teach evangelists how they fit within the grand picture of the kingdom, pastors will teach evangelists how they fit within community.

We can clearly see that pastors and evangelists bring health to one another. When pastors and evangelists work together, pastors begin to play a key role to relationally disciple those who evangelists are bringing to the Lord.

Pastors and Teachers

Just as apostles and prophets are a ministerial match made in heaven, so are pastors and teachers. In fact, we can see in more conservative church settings, it is quite common to see pastors and teachers working together. While both apostles and prophets have a primary focus on the grander vision of what God desires on a mass scale, teachers and pastors have a mandate to the individuals in the church.

Similar to pastors, teachers in many ways have a shepherding heart to protect the sheep. While pastors have a heart to protect individuals in the realm of emotions and relationships, teachers have a burden to protect people's minds from unhealthy doctrines and theologies. Pastors and teachers co-labour together to protect God's people, so they can grow up healthily to a place of maturity.

The pitfall that can comes with pastors and teachers working together, is that it can be hard for other facets of the five-fold ministry to fit in amongst this dynamic-duo. We often see teachers functioning under the covering of pastors, which will often result in apostles, prophets, and evangelists not having their hand in what is being built. This happens because the pastoral and teacher heart to protect people can easily be brought to an extreme in being overly protective, even to the point of being cautious concerning the things of Holy Spirit. Teachers and pastors function at their healthiest under the accountability of an apostolic leader. Apostles can teach pastors and teachers how to function healthily with those who have different callings or giftings, so that they can be part of the greater expression of what God is doing in the earth.

PASTORAL PRAYER

If you have a heart to grow in your relationship with Jesus the Pastor, pray this prayer with me:

"Jesus, I receive You as my Pastor. Teach me to encounter Your pastoral heart for me. I receive You in the deep places of my soul to bring healing and freedom. I embrace You as my Counsellor. Free me from any fear, anxieties, or insecurities that may exist in my heart. Teach me what healthy community looks like. I pray for a revelation of belonging. Show me where I fit within the family of God. Thank you for being by Guard, Protector, and Shield."

OFFICE OF A
TEACHER

Every word written in the Bible is an open door for us to come into a revelatory encounter with Jesus.

DEFINING A
TEACHER

A teacher's function in the body of Christ is primarily operating as the mind of the church. One of the reasons God has stationed teachers as part of the five-fold ministry is to get people rooted in the written word of God. There is a grace over teachers to receive and release the ministry of the Spirit of Wisdom, Revelation, and Knowledge. This means they can pull pivotal truths out of the word of God with ease and present it with authority.

The book of Acts and some of Paul's epistles mention a man named Apollos, who had the reputation of being a prominent teacher back in the early church. Paul said in 1 Corinthians 3:6 that as an apostle he would plant, and Apollos would water the church through his teachings because he was a man of a fervent spirit and eloquence (Acts 18:25-26).

Teachers possess a natural ability to take heavenly principles and to explain them in a way that people will be able to understand. When Jesus walked the earth He often taught in parables. I believe He did this for two reasons: the first reason was because He wanted to hide the truth from the proud. Jesus would teach revelation through parables, knowing that only those who were humble and hungry enough to seek understanding would find the truth. The second reason why He spoke in parables was because He was trying to teach people heavenly principles, and He had to use a language that they would understand. He couldn't approach the masses by talking about the kingdom of heaven the way He personally experienced it, because they would have had no grid of comparison to understand what He was saying. This is why He would compare the kingdom of heaven to something such as farming, which was a common industry in that culture. As a master Teacher, Jesus met people where they were at. Teachers have the ability to take profound truths from the scriptures and explain them in a way where whoever they are speaking to will comprehend. They demystify spiritual principles, making them accessible to everyone.

In my opinion, it is necessary to receive from multiple teachers since we understand in part. It is beneficial for many teachers to be receiving and teaching revelation because then we have a far broader stroke of truth being covered, rather than only having one teacher who is expected to have a full revelation of all things.

While I wouldn't consider myself a five-fold teacher, I do know that I carry a gift of teaching. Several years ago, I had a very interesting experience. I was driving in my vehicle in the country praying, when something very interesting happened. It felt as though I could feel a healing anointing entering my car. Considering my wife and I have seen many healings in our ministry, I have a huge value for the Lord showing up in such a way.

I asked the Lord, "What type of healing anointing is this? Is it for physical healing? Inner-healing? Healing of the mind?"

Immediately, Holy Spirit spoke to me saying, "This anointing is for brining healing to people's doctrines." He then began speaking to me about the teaching anointing being restored to the church. My mind was blown, to say the least.

I truly believe there is a significant wave of teaching we are about to experience in the body of Christ. Over the years, I've had the great privilege of getting to speak with many leaders and pastors who are more conservative, training them in the things of the Spirit. Probably the main tool I use to equip them is through the teaching anointing. Many of us assume those in more conservative circles are completely opposed to the things of the Spirit; while this might be true on occasion, often it's not.

What we often don't realize, is that more charismatic churches are often led by apostles or prophets, who may not gear towards teaching. Therefore, profound manifestations of the Spirit take place, yet there may not be an extreme emphasis on biblical explanation. In my experience, many leaders in more conservative churches aren't opposed to the things of the Spirit; they just have a very high value for truth, and want to see how things are biblical and why they are beneficial. In my teaching ministry, I often biblically unpack the supernatural to show it is scriptural and beneficial. I'm continually impacted at the amount of conservative churches and leaders who have embraced the supernatural things of God through use of the teaching gift.

While connecting and working with many teachers, I've noticed three key functions that someone who walks in the office of a teacher will exemplify:

Teachers Train

Just like every facet of the five-fold ministry, a teacher's job is to equip the saints for the work of ministry. Teachers equip the church by teaching scripture, but they are also called to train the rest of the body of Christ how to tap into revelation as easily as they themselves do. I believe this is a crucial part of this office, otherwise a congregation's spiritual food will only come secondhand from the teacher. We all need to know how to encounter Jesus through the written word of God. It doesn't matter if we are a leader in the church, in business, or a high school student; if we are children of God we need to be deeply rooted in the Bible.

I have a good friend who I believe walks in the office of a teacher. One of his functions is that he actually teaches people to read the Bible. He is by far one of the most biblically knowledgeable people I've ever met. While he teaches, I've watched him take the simplest of scriptures and pull the most radical revelations from it. Not only does he know how to unpack the word of God, but he then shows his students how they can receive similar revelation. As a teacher, he doesn't only teach from the word, he shows that it is a tool through which we can all encounter the heart of God.

Hebrews 4:12: "For the word of God is living and powerful, and sharper than any two-edged sword, piercing even to the division of soul and spirit, and of joints and marrow, and is a discerner of the thoughts and intents of the heart."

The Greek word for "word" in this verse is *logos*, which is referring to the written word of God. God's word is living and active. It is good news that the Bible is not a dead word. It is alive because it is God-breathed. Every word and verse in the Bible is an open heaven for us to come into a revelatory encounter with Jesus. Teachers play a key role in our growth by not only teaching us truths from the Bible, but by also showing us how to read scripture with Holy Spirit so we can encounter the heart of God through His word.

Teachers Disciple

One of my favourite characteristics about teachers is their ability to disciple. While evangelists and evangelistic people can help birth people into the kingdom, I'm certain that pastors and teachers are the key to supernatural growth for someone newly saved. Many second-generation Christians grow up going to Sunday school, learning all the basic truths and stories in the Bible. Stories such as Noah's ark and Daniel in the lion's den are carved within their very foundation of understanding. However, this often isn't true for someone who is introduced to Jesus much later on in life.

I remember when I first met the Lord at the age of sixteen, I was brand new to everything God related. I stepped out from the kingdom of darkness, a place filled with pain, abuse, and addiction, into the kingdom of light. Experiencing the goodness of God was a complete culture shock to me. While the church I got saved in wasn't experiencing a lot concerning the supernatural manifestations of Holy Spirit, they were deeply rooted in the written word of God. This permitted me to receive from several teachers at the church who were able to get me rooted in the foundations of the kingdom of God. They saturated me with scripture and teachings, helping to shape a biblical foundation for me. In my earlier years, their knowledge of the word of God pushed me into accelerated growth. To this day, I am tremendously grateful for the ministry of teachers in my life from when I first met the Lord.

Teachers Guard Doctrine

I have found it incredibly necessary to surround myself with teachers. In many ways, they are a doctrinal plumb-line keeping us in proper theological order. One of the anointings over my life is one of a forerunner. This means God shares biblical truths with me that aren't yet wide-spread, and I get to forerun these truths through teaching making them more common. That being said, I have a very high value for truth, so I've found it beneficial to surround myself with teachers who are sound in the word of God. When I get a new revelation from the Lord, before I begin teaching it, I will often run it by a five-fold teacher who I'm in relationship with. I even do this with the books I write. Every book goes through various stages of editing. For my books, I will often even send them through theological edits before they are published. A five-fold teacher will read through, making sure what I'm teaching is doctrinally sound. I don't do this because I undervalue my ability to understand God's word; I do it because I value the office and gifts of teachers. I recognize that God has gifted the different parts of the church accordingly.

I remember several years ago when I was the associate pastor of a church, we had a particular five-fold teacher on our team. This man was highly knowledgeable in scripture. In our church, there was a network of house churches where numerous leaders would teach week-by-week. At one point, there was a form of false doctrine that was taught in one of the house churches. Without us realizing, this doctrine swept throughout the grander group of congregants. I remember when I first heard of the false teaching, my discernment was ringing off the hook; however, as a team we couldn't quite place why the teaching was off biblically. This was where the teacher came in. He showed us all biblically why this teaching was unscriptural, as well as what the effects of this teaching would be if it continued being taught in our church. Trusting his gift, we were able to teach our people the dangers of this particular false doctrine, preventing this harmful theology from taking root.

Healthy theology doesn't only revolve around Jesus; it is completely saturated in Him. Teachers keep us in a healthy balance doctrinally, so that everything we believe reflects the heart of God and is founded scripturally. Just as pastors guard the church, keeping us healthy in our soul and within community, teachers guard the mind of the church, rooting us in truth.

COMMON PITFALLS
OF TEACHERS

The teaching ministry is an irreplaceable part of God's kingdom. However, if we are going to see it utilized to its full expression, we need to be aware of its potential pitfalls. Just like every ministry, it is beneficial when it is healthy, however it can also cause hurt and pain if it's not wielded with love and integrity. Over the years, I've worked with teachers all over the world. They've helped shed light for me to understand what pitfalls can follow the teaching ministry. Some of these pitfalls are struggles they've observed with others, as well as some they've personally learned to overcome.

Here are some pitfalls that can be experienced by teachers and those who are highly teacher-like in their gifting:

Intellectual Pride

Every five-fold teacher I've ever met has had a gifted mind. It makes sense considering how they can dissect scripture. In many ways they seem like a boundless well of knowledge. That being said, those who encounter God in such a way need to remember to guard their heart from intellectual pride.

1 Corinthians 8:1: "Knowledge puffs up, but love edifies."

We need to understand something; knowledge in and of itself isn't bad. We know this because Isaiah 11:2 talks about how the spirit of knowledge rested upon Jesus. Therefore, knowledge is clearly something we should desire to grow in. The reason Paul wrote saying, "Knowledge puffs up" is because knowledge apart from revelation can make us arrogant. Every one of us needs to be a place where knowledge, wisdom, and revelation all meet. Let's take a look at the difference between all three:

While knowledge is understanding something with our mind, revelation is understanding something with our heart. Wisdom in many ways is knowing how to apply both knowledge and revelation appropriately. Together knowledge, revelation, and wisdom are a trinity of understanding. If we are not willing to grow in all three, then we risk leaving an empty seat for ignorance to fill.

If we are only growing in knowledge, we can end up being far too intellectual in our faith. The last thing we should ever want is to only know *about* Jesus. I don't want to just know about Him. I want to know Him deeply. I don't just want knowledge of Him in my mind; I want a heart revelation!

Knowledge puffs up, but love edifies. Love edifies because it's an encounter. It transitions us from the place of knowledge to revelation. Those gifted as teachers need to remember to allow their knowledge of Him to sink deep into their hearts. We need to always remember that a theory about God will help us shape an opinion, whereas an encounter with Him truly transforms us.

Legalism

Something I absolutely love about teachers is that their understanding of scripture empowers them to adamantly stand for truth. A teacher's knowledge of the Bible helps bring purity to the body of Christ. It instills a standard of holiness.

I'll start this off by saying this: I absolutely love the revelation of holiness. I love the fear of the Lord. I teach on these topics regularly. If you've followed my teachings throughout the years, you would know I have a very high standard and value for Godly character and integrity. However, holiness needs to be partnered with a revelation of grace. They go hand-in-hand; we cannot separate them. When we campout in extremes concerning holiness, we can end up robbing people from being on a journey. We expect immediate perfection from people instead of allowing them time to grow, working out their salvation. This is where we transition from a revelation of holiness, to the pitfall of legalism.

Here's an example of how someone might think if they battle mentalities of legalism:

Say there is someone who is a newer believer who struggles with something like pornography. We obviously know pornography is not good. It's highly destructive. It is sin. Someone who perhaps battles mentalities of legalism and knows scripture well, might think something like, "Scripture says looking upon someone lustfully is sin, so they best stop." This is true. They should try to stop. However, giving up an addiction is often more of a journey rather than a quick fix, especially for someone who has just met the Lord. A teacher may be able to see the black and white rules of the kingdom, yet they need to also see the value of the journey of others. There needs to be grace for growth. When we slip into mentalities of legalism, we could end up looking poised on the outside, but still be shattered in our heart. This is the result of simply applying rules without allowing Jesus the time to come and heal out heart.

Expecting change in actions apart from a heart transformation doesn't often go very far. Something like pornography isn't just a habit that needs adjusting. It's rooted from wounding in the soul. Someone who has a severe addiction like this might need to journey out from their addiction. They may likely need to go through deliverance, inner healing, or counselling.

While teachers can struggle with the extremes of holiness, pastors can fall in to the extreme ends of grace. An extreme grace mentality is a form of passivity, permitting people to campout in sin instead of championing and affirming them to rise higher. This is why teachers and pastors need to work together. They balance one another out. Teachers raise the bar of what biblical holiness looks like, while pastors establish a value for extending grace throughout people's journey.

Criticism Towards the New Things of God

In 2 Kings 1, there was a very interesting move of God taking place. It was an emergence of an unusual amount of prophets being risen up. There was never another time recorded in scripture when this many prophets were accompanied together. We see a very similar occurrence taking place in the time-period when Jesus walked the earth. However, this time it wasn't a vast amount of prophets who were risen up. Instead there was an emergence of those gifted as teachers. The entire culture of Israel in this time revolved around understanding Moses' writings and keeping Israel's customs. Pharisees were considered experts of the law. They were essentially the teachers "Rabbis" of that time-period.

We need to understand something here. The Pharisees of this time weren't always in essence "bad" people. We can certainly see how they went down a dark road, but they did do some good for God's kingdom. These religious leaders were the ones who preserved Old Testament scriptures for hundreds of years until Christ's coming. They made sure Israel kept in accordance with the word of God. What made them corrupt was their response to Jesus. The Pharisees were so entrenched within tradition, that they completely missed the Lord when He came. So much so, that they were the ones who enforced His crucifixion.

This is a perfect scriptural example of what happens if we hold tradition above experience with the Lord. This is often where many get stuck concerning their revelatory maturity. We grow accustomed to past truths, therefore fear pursuing new ones.

The Pharisees expected a Messiah to come. They tried to interpret the scriptures and created a box of expectancy in their minds of what they thought the Messiah should look like. Jesus came to earth and was so confident in who He was that He would not try to awkwardly squeeze into their box. In fact, He completely abolished their box of expectation. Jesus is the great I AM because He is completely confident in who He is, not willing to compromise Himself. I always hear people say, "We should not put God in a box." When in actuality, God hasn't been in a box since the Old Testament when He dwelled in the Ark of the Covenant. God is too big to box up. We are the ones who have been barricaded and caged from truth by an unhealthy soul-tie to familiarity. We need to heed wisdom by learning to step beyond what is comfortable to us. A past revelation can cradle us for a time, but as we grow older we need to step beyond our cribs to expand our knowledge of kingdom life. God's heart is a vast place waiting to be discovered.

Doctrine and theology should not be used as a box to intellectualize our relationship with God. They should be used as tools to guide us into the depths of His heart. Healthy theology and doctrine will encourage us to dive into God's relational nature. Healthy theology encourages us to step beyond intellectual understanding into the place of encounter.

We need those who are gifted as teachers. However, we need teachers who are postured in humility so they can adjust as the Lord begins to do something new. In John 2, there was a Pharisee named Nicodemus. This man, instead of criticizing Jesus, postured Himself in humility. We can see all throughout these verses that he probed Jesus with questions in pursuit of truth. These are the types of teachers we need; ones who are students to the Teacher of teachers.

Divisiveness

While teachers play a prominent role in guarding the theological health of the church, it's important that theology isn't used as a tool to bring division. Sometimes when people have a strong stance on certain theologies, opinion can have a tendency to trump relationship.

Personally, I'm a very firm believer in honouring people well. I believe it's a prominent key of the kingdom of God. I have friends in ministry where we blatantly disagree with one another concerning some of our views on theology. However, we never let our views on secondary and tertiary doctrines become a wedge in relationship. I have ministry friends who are Baptists, Pentecostals, Alliance, Charismatic, etc. Our views may differ on topics such as tongues, eschatology, and the things of the Spirit; however, we have learned how to meet around Jesus who is our primary doctrine. I have learned that denominational walls are irrelevant when we have created a culture of honour in our relationships. I believe Holy Spirit is training believers to look over denominational walls to see the hearts of genuine people who love God with all that they are.

It's true that the word of God is a weapon. However, it's a weapon against the enemy, not against people. We need to always remember to be honouring towards those who differ from us in theology.

Performance and Striving

Just like with every giftset, if we aren't finding our identity in the Lord we will often try to find our value in what we are good at. The same can be said of teachers. A teacher who isn't secure in who they are in the Lord, may try to find their worth in what they know. This can unfortunately result in an irrational pursuit of knowledge. Not only can this turn into performance and striving to impress God and people, it can also lead to competition with other teachers.

Based on my experience with teachers, they will often specialize in specific topics. Considering how vast the kingdom of heaven is, how could they not? Therefore, I know specific teachers who primarily teach church history. I know others who focus their energies on teaching others to read the word of God, or on learning Hebrew and Aramaic. A teacher needs to discern what area the Lord wants them to specialize in, otherwise they risk spreading themselves far too thin. A teacher who has slipped into performance, may try to overextend themselves into studying and teaching what is outside of their grace.

As I mentioned before, I don't believe I'm a five-fold teacher, but I love the word of God. I love studying and diving into new truths. That said, to guard myself from overextending myself in my studies, I have a standard rule for myself. I will not study what won't change the way I live my life for the better; and I won't teach what the Lord hasn't released me to teach. I can't count how many speaking engagements I've turned down because I was asked to train on what isn't my grace. It's not that I disagree with those topics; I just want to stay in my own lane that the Lord has paved for me. I don't want performance and striving to spread me too thin.

When we refuse to stay in our own lane, we end up settling for becoming a jack of all trades instead of learning to walk in excellence with what the Lord has entrusted to us. Striving and performance can direct us in far too many directions. Instead of following the will of my insecurities, I would rather follow the will of the Lord. This is what keeps us on track. It's what steers us away from competition and comparison. It focuses us, so we can fulfill our God-given mandate.

How Teachers Fit in the Five-Fold

We need the entire five-fold ministry operating in unity within the church, otherwise we risk building something for God that is unbalanced. Ephesians 2:20 talks about how the household of God (the church) is built upon the foundation of the apostles and prophets. You could say, Jesus the solid rock (Matthew 7:24-27) is presented by the evangelists. Upon the solid rock, the foundation is built by the apostles and prophets. Upon the foundation, the household of God is built and shaped by pastors and teachers. We can see that if we want to build for God's kingdom with lasting significance, then we need to see the fullness of God's leadership not only in action, but functioning in unity.

With every five-fold office there are strengths as well as blind spots. This is why God has called the five-fold ministry to work together as a team, instead of independently. In this chapter, I would like to shed light concerning how some of these different offices can work together with the office of a teacher, how they complement one another, and what tensions may exist between them.

Teachers and Apostles

1 Corinthians 12:28: "And God has appointed these in the church: first apostles, second prophets, third teachers, after that miracles, then gifts of healings, helps, administrations, varieties of tongues."

Apostles and teachers are called to co-labour together in a very interesting way. In 1 Corinthians 12:28, there is an interesting order that Paul uses while listing who God has appointed in the church. God appoints, first apostles, second prophets, and third teachers. Apostles and prophets, God's first and second appointed, are often focused on bridging heaven to earth. When this happens, revival atmosphere is created; the supernatural occurs. God thirdly appoints the teacher, which is crucial if we are to see healthy kingdom culture. While apostles and prophets help bridge heaven to earth, teachers will play a role of training the church to understand how the move of the Spirit is both biblical and from the heart of God. While apostles and prophets are focused on what God is doing, teachers are focused on how people are responding to what God is doing. Teachers have the ability to biblically, practically, and intellectually unpack what is happening in the supernatural realm.

This way, everyone is able to comprehend what the Lord is doing.

I have seen times when the Lord is pouring out supernaturally through either an apostolic or prophetic leader in a church meeting; however, what the Lord was doing wasn't received by a large amount of people in the service. This was actually because there was no one there with a teaching anointing to articulate properly was taking place. Teachers partnering with apostolic leaders helps demystify the things of the Spirit, so they become accessible and comprehendible to everyone.

Teachers can also benefit apostles by helping communicate the apostolic vision to the people they are called to lead. Sometimes since apostles have vision for the masses, they have troubles communicating to the individual. This is where teachers can come in. Teachers can help an apostle not only to communicate their vision, but also to explain to the people how they fit into the grander vision as individuals.

Teachers and Prophets

In my opinion, prophets and teachers working together is a necessity. It is prophets who establish the value of the spoken word of God, and teachers enforce the value of the written word of God. Both are needed. Period.

There is an obvious tension between prophets and teachers. Prophets are more geared towards things that are potently spiritual and supernatural, whereas teachers are geared more towards analysis and intellectualism. While there is distinct contrast here, I believe God has created both offices with extreme strengths that cover one another's weaknesses.

Teachers assist prophets by keeping them grounded. I have met prophets who carry profound teaching gifts, and it is often crucial that they can bounce their new revelation and teachings off of Spirit-led teachers. I have seen prophets who try to teach apart from this form of accountability go down dark paths of false doctrines. This is one of the many reasons why prophets need to be relationally connected with teachers.

Teachers will also play a big role in helping prophets communicate the word of the Lord. Often, a prophet's priority is to receive the word of the Lord, and then to communicate it. Since this is a prophet's job, based on how they communicate, some may catch the word of the Lord while others may not. A teacher's job is more than just communicating a message; it is to make sure people understand the message. Teachers play a role in helping to demystify the prophetic word of the Lord so that it becomes palatable for everyone.

Another reason why prophets and teachers need to receive from one another is because prophets help train teachers not to become too intellectually dependent. When teachers are only intellectually dependent, they can have a tendency to dismiss anything that God may do that does not fit into their intellectual grid. This is dangerous, because then we risk reasoning ourselves out of experiencing what God may be doing. Prophets help equip teachers in how to allow the written word of God inside of them to become alive and active. Prophets guide teachers in how to marry their intellectual gifts with the gifts of the Spirit.

Teachers and Evangelists

Even though the function of evangelists and teachers look completely different, they are greatly complimentary to one another. One of the tension points between evangelists and teachers lies with the fact that their individual roles are on the opposite ends of the spectrum. Evangelists thrive in the place of risk. They are moved by passion to see people encounter the supernatural love of God outside the church. Teachers are often quite intellectual in how they understand the things of God. Therefore, they will often be more utilized by God within the four walls of the church. Even though they are different, both roles are irreplaceable in the kingdom of God and are very beneficial to one another.

While evangelists are often focused on those who do not know Jesus, teachers take a role of equipping individuals once they transition into knowing Christ. As evangelists and teachers begin to work alongside one another, not only do we see people saved, but we see them discipled. As evangelists are playing a role in bringing people to the Lord, teachers can then begin to teach these people the foundation truths of God. This leads them into allowing the Lord by laying a foundation of who He is in their lives. Teachers working with those who are new to knowing God, quickens them to a place of maturity.

Teachers and Pastors

Just as apostles and prophets are a ministerial match made in heaven, so are pastors and teachers. In fact, we can see in more conservative church settings, it is quite common to see pastors and teachers working together. While both apostles and prophets have a primary focus on the grander vision of what God desires on a mass scale, teachers and pastors have a mandate to the individuals in the church.

Similar to pastors, teachers in many ways have a shepherding heart to protect the sheep. While pastors have a heart to protect individuals in the realm of emotions and relationships, teachers have a burden to protect people's minds from unhealthy doctrines and theologies. Pastors and teachers co-labour together to protect God's people, so they can grow up healthily to a place of maturity.

The pitfall that can comes with pastors and teachers working together, is that it can be hard for other facets of the five-fold ministry to fit in amongst this dynamic-duo. We often see teachers functioning under the covering of pastors, which will often result in apostles, prophets, and evangelists not having their hand in what is being built. This happens because the pastoral and teacher heart to protect people can easily be brought to an extreme in being overly protective, even to the point of being cautious concerning the things of Holy Spirit. Teachers and pastors function at their healthiest under the accountability of an apostolic leader. Apostles can teach pastors and teachers how to function healthily with those who have different callings or giftings, so that they can be part of the greater expression of what God is doing in the earth.

TEACHER PRAYER

If you have a heart to grow deeper in relationship with Jesus the Teacher, pray this prayer with me:

"Jesus, I receive You as my Teacher. I pray that You will open the mysteries of Your word to me. Give me a hunger for Your word; a hunger for truth. I ask for knowledge, wisdom, and revelation of You and Your ways. I pray that You use my life, work, family, and relationships as a tool to teach me. Train me, Lord. Equip me. Refine me."

Conclusion

We are amidst a pivotal reformation in the church. No matter who you are reading this book, you are called by God. You have been strategically placed by the Lord to be a bridge for His unconditional love to invade the lives of those around you. God is taking the church from the corner of the field, to the centre stage of the world. He is training the church to not sit on the sidelines, to passively watch the world change around us. He is showing us how to stand victoriously in the nations. He is raising us up to walk out our mandate, to expand the kingdom of God throughout the earth in every stream of society. This is why we need to be equipped.

Take a look at this portion of scripture with me:

Ephesians 6:10-18: "Finally, my brethren, be strong in the Lord and in the power of His might. Put on the whole armor of God, that you may be able to stand against the wiles of the devil. For we do not wrestle against flesh and blood, but against principalities, against powers, against the rulers of the darkness of this age, against spiritual hosts of wickedness in the heavenly places. Therefore take up the whole armor of God, that you may be able to withstand in the evil day, and having done all, to stand. Stand therefore, having girded your waist with truth, having put on the breastplate of righteousness, and having shod your feet with the preparation of the gospel of peace; above all, taking the shield of faith with which you will be able to quench all the fiery darts of the wicked one. And take the helmet of salvation, and the sword of the Spirit, which is the word of God; praying always with all prayer and supplication in the Spirit, being watchful to this end with all perseverance and supplication for all the saints."

We are all called to take up the armour of God, to be prepared to live out the mandate over our lives. In many ways the five-fold ministry helps us to be better equipped with the armour of God. Apostles help secure us in our helmets of salvation and our breastplates of righteousness. Prophets play a part in teaching us to wield the sword of the Spirit, which is the word of God. Evangelists function in helping to shod our feet with the preparation of the gospel. Pastors equip us with the shield of faith to quench the fiery darts of the enemy. Teachers help gird our waist with the belt of truth, keeping us in balance and order.

Jesus is making Himself known as the Apostle, Prophet, Evangelist, Pastor, and Teacher. He is raising up individuals who known how to receive kingdom vision for their spheres of influence. He's raising up prophetic mouthpieces who speak His word in even some of the darkest places. He's infusing us with boldness, to release an evangelistic roar. He's raising up those who understand healthy relationships; those with pastoral hearts to minister to those hurting. He's calling us to be grounded in truth, engulfed in the word of God. Our job is to receive Him in totality.

If you are readying this, whether you are a five-fold minister, or someone who is called to other realms of influence, remember that you are called by the very voice of God. Don't step into mindsets of belittling who you are called to be. In fact, if you have ever felt like the last choice, then you are the perfect candidate to do remarkable things. God has a reputation for picking those who feel like they aren't capable; He picks them, befriends them, and turns them into someone powerful. He is there for us throughout the whole story of our lives. He chooses us in our weakness and refines us to be strong in Him. He calls us when we are dependent on ourselves and others, and teaches us to be dependent on Him. I am so thankful that God chose Peter, the coward, and turned him into Peter, the apostle. I am so thankful that God called Matthew, the tax collector, and turned him into an apostle and author of one of the gospels. God chose Moses, the murderer, and turned him into a man who delivered a nation. God chose David, an adulterer, and made him one of the greatest kings who ever lived. God chooses the least likely and uses them to do remarkable things (1 Corinthians 1:27).

Look at this story from Mark 10:35-40 with me:

In this story, James and John asked Jesus if they could be seated on thrones to Jesus' right and left in the kingdom of heaven. When they did so, it seemed as though they were throwing out their most far-fetched idea and desire. We look at what they asked as though it was ridiculous to ask such an extreme request. Little did they know, the Father had a greater reward for those who are in Christ. As to whether we are to sit on Jesus' right or left in glory is undefined; however, what is clear in scripture is that we are seated on His throne with Him, which is by far better (Ephesians 2:6, Revelation 3:21). In Christ we are seated with Jesus on His throne to rule and reign with Him, in relationship with Him. John and James' loftiest request to sit beside Jesus hardly compared to the goodness of what God actually had planned for them, which was to be seated *with* Him.

Ephesians 3:20: "Now to Him who is able to do exceedingly abundantly above all that we ask or think, according to the power that works in us."

Sow in faith to God your greatest desires and most far-fetched ideas, believing that He can dream bigger than you can in what He will accomplish both in and through your life. He has plans for your life that will blow your mind. Remember, if we believe we are powerless, insignificant or unimportant, then we are living in a defeated mentality. God wants to break us out of identity crisis by shaping within us a victorious perspective of ourselves. Always remember that you play an integral role in what God is doing throughout the earth. You are not called on the sidelines. You are pivotal to His plan and irreplaceable in His heart.

"Jesus, we receive you as our great Apostle, Prophet, Evangelist, Pastor, and Teacher. Let the full expression of who you are to be shaped with us. We want to know you in full. We pray this in your powerful name."

Made in the USA
San Bernardino, CA
19 December 2019